Tails
and the
Unexpected

Tails
and the
Unexpected
A Collection of Unusual Angling Stories

Edited by
BILLEE CHAPMAN PINCHER

SWAN·HILL
PRESS

First published in the UK in 1995
by Swan Hill Press, an imprint of Airlife Publishing Ltd

British Library Cataloguing in Publication Data
  A catalogue record for this book
  is available from the British Library

ISBN 1 85310 549 X

Typeset by Hewer Text Composition Services, Edinburgh
Printed in England by Biddles Ltd., Guildford and King's Lynn

Swan Hill Press
an imprint of Airlife Publishing Ltd
101 Longden Road, Shrewsbury SY3 9EB

Contents

Foreword

As my dear, late friend Sir Thomas Sopwith was wont to say, fishing is the only sport where there are no rules – meaning that nowhere else is the unexpected encountered so frequently or in such variety. Anything can happen out fishing – and often does, to such an extent that, down the centuries, non-fishers have cast doubt on our credibility, leading to such questions as 'Are all fishermen liars or do all liars fish?' Partly to counter this calumny by providing a genuine record of unusual angling experiences, but mainly to provide an interesting and amusing read, I have been collecting true anecdotes from anglers of all types over several years, publishing a selection of them under the title *Fish Tales* in 1989. As evidence of their authenticity, they were all presented under the names of those who had supplied them.

Since then, many more true stories have been given to me by anglers whom I have met, who have been stimulated to contact me after reading *Fish Tales* or to whom I have written myself. Many of them fully justify the title of this second book, in which I have widened the scope to include more about coarse fish and sea fish.

Billee Chapman Pincher
Kintbury, Berks.
1995

Those Involved

Ainslie, Mr Pat
Aldrich, Bernard
Allaman, Ted
Anderson, Ian
Archer, Jeremy
Astor, Richard
Atkinson, Sir Robert
Attlee, Lord
Bailey, Bob
Banner, Sir Harmood
Bates, Alfred
Batho, Tom
Beare, Robin
Beaverbrook, Lord
Benjamin, Ron
Benney, Gerald
Blake, George
Bowman, Sir John
Brabourne, Lord
Breden, Robert
Brodrick, George
Broughton, Dr R.B.
Browse, David
Bush, Roy
Channing-Williams, David
Chapel, Dr Andrew
Christie, Katriona
Church, Bob
Clifford-Jones, Nevile
Cockwill, Peter
Coen, Cavaliere del Lavoro
    Massimo
Deterding, Shirley
Dido
Douglas, Kirk
Drewett, John
Edmonds, R.
Edwards, R.
Evans, John
Evanson, Richard
Faldo, Nick
Farley, Philip
Farnell, Colin
Farrant, John
Farrer, Mark
Fraser, Malcolm
Forrester, Donald
Gardiner, David

Garvan, Peter
Gilmour, Sue
Grant, Bob
Griggs, Annie
Gundry, Rose
Hadow, Sir Michael
Hall, Peter
Hammond, Ray
Haston, Richard
Hicks, Andrew
Hill-Trevor, Hon Charles
Home of the Hirsel, Earl
Hounslow, Jeff
Huddy, Philip
Hunt, Sir Rex
Ingram, Tony
Jackson, Nigel
Jessett, Andy
Johnson, George
Jones, Stephen
Katemba, John
Kelton, Michael
Keswick, Sir Chippendale
Klootwijk, James
Laing, Lady Marian
Lewando, Sir Jan
Lloyd-Price, Mark
Long, Dr John
Lyne, Peter
Macer-Wright, Don
Mackenzie, Vice-Admiral Sir
    Hugh
Mann, Margaret
Marber, Stanley
Marshall, Robert
Maxwell, Robert
McGuinness, Brian
McKenzie, Bruce
Morris, Bob
Mountain, Sir Denis
Mountbatten, Earl
Newlands, Mickey
Noble, John
Parry, Michael
Penney, Bruce
Penny, Stephen
Phipps, Dave
Porter, Dame Shirley

Porter, Martin
Pratt, Caroline
Quinn, Tom
Rattray, Robert
Richards, Tony
Roberts, John
Rodgers, Sid
Rogoff, Graham
Rowcliffe, Lilla
Rushmer, Bill
Samuel, Tony
Santa Cruz,
    Sebastian
Sautell Senior, John
Selby, Dr Leonard
Sergeant, Roger
Shaw, David
Sieff, Lord
Simpkiss, Dr Michael
Sinclair, Norman
Smith, Sir Alan
Smith, Michael
Sopwith, Sir Thomas
Speer, Keith
Spicer, Keith
Spiers, Bob
Stansfeld, Major
    Anthony
Stevenson, Michael
Stirling, Joe
Stevenson, Michael
Thorburn, Eric
Tritton, Jim
van der Byl, Senator P.K.
Venables, Bernard
Waddington, Richard
Ward, Connie
Warrin, Richard
Wellington, Duke of
White, Kenny
Whitcombe, Art
Wieser, Dick
Willis, George
Wills, Sir Seton
Wilson, Dermot
Wilson, Stan
Woodward, Lynn
Woolnough, Peter

Chapter 1

Titanic Battle

Anyone who has caught a 43-pound salmon in Scotland should, surely, be judged fortunate; but supposing he has also hooked and played a fish which might well have beaten the long-established record of 64 pounds and then lost it? I suspect that this is what may have happened to my friend Michael Smith, who owned the Dalguise beat of the Tay. He makes no such claim himself but his account of his struggle with the monster, written shortly after its end, describes the longest, toughest and most determined fight, by both salmon and angler, that I have ever heard of, and I am privileged to put it on permanent record. I was first made aware of it by a lady who had seen a copy of Michael's hand-written account of his battle when fishing the River Beauly, where it occurred. Only when I asked Michael about it did I receive a copy of the saga from him. It is dated 11 September 1986.

At 9.15 am I dropped my former father-in-law, Bill Hatten, off at the island above the Breeches, after pointing out some likely spots. I parked my car at the Minister pool and, as the water was low, I took my 10-foot Bruce and Walker carbon rod, leaving my longer rod behind. The reel carried 30 yards of slow-sink line and about 80 yards of 15 pound backing. The cast was of 10 pound breaking strain and had a Collie Dog fly on the tail and a Shrimp fly on the bob. I waded out above the Minister to come down on good lies to the left and right of me. While casting to the right, working the flies over the ledge, I experienced a vicious take. The fish showed its side and I thought, 'Good! It's 30–35 pounds plus and fresh.' The time was 9.30 and the fish began a long run towards the tail of the pool. I too ran, knee-deep, towards the right bank but could follow no further as the big, round stones gave way to deep water. My backing ran out to the drum and a break followed.

On winding in I discovered that my backing had broken, leaving the line and some 50 yards of light-coloured braided nylon attached to the fish. I quickly waded back up and out and drove rapidly up to Bill at the island. He dropped everything and jumped into my car. We then took the boat out and scoured the bottom. Over on the far side, trailing in 10 feet of water, we located the backing. I threaded up what remained of the backing on my reel, attached a General Practitioner fly to it, hooked the missing backing at the first cast and retied it to what was on my reel. On winding up I was surprised and delighted to discover that the fish was still on. The time was 9.45.

For the next two hours the fish led us a merry dance. It did not rush but it did not stop. It would travel up to the fence on the bank and back to the tail of the pool. Twice I went ashore below the fence to try walking the fish into shallow water, but it would have none of it. I got Bill to get a flask of coffee from the car and, after a drink, we changed tactics, taking the boat to the dead water off the right bank in the hope of drowning the fish. While trying this for the third time the fish ran into the glide at the tail of the pool and we followed. When it appeared to be making for the Piles pool below I jumped out to follow. At the last minute it turned and, leaving a big wake, headed upstream. The boat was out of control and I was on the rocks 10 yards away. When I ran out of line and backing I threw the rod into the water and grabbed the boat, turning its head into the stream. It was now midday.

When Bill got the oars to bite I jumped into the stern and we saw the rod in the stones at the tail of the Minister and realised that the fish was away. On retrieving the rod, we saw that the backing had broken again, but nearer the end of the reel than the last time. We scoured the tail of the pool but could not find the line and I was for giving up, but not Bill. I suggested that the last chance might be at the head of the pool in the fish's original lie. It was now 12.30 and we rowed up, rather disconsolately, realising that the hydroelectric station higher up would soon be generating, creating a rise in the water which would ruin our hopes. The light was also bad.

Opposite the fence where my car was parked I spotted the backing and, after successfully repeating the hooking procedure, the battle was on again. Once more, the fish ran back to the tail of the pool with us in pursuit in the boat. The fish turned and jumped and I saw him clearly – a huge head, white underneath and then the tail smacking the surface. I said to Bill, 'Christ! I thought he was big but he is bloody massive!'

At 1.45 pm – more than four hours after I had hooked the salmon – the fish ran up and down the pool about four times and twice we took him across to the dead water where, still in the boat, we tried to get on top of him and raise him within gaffing distance. No joy! The fish ran back to the neck of the Minister while we took the boat into the slack, midstream. We were in a routine by now. The hydro had given us about 12 inches more water and we kept up with the fish for a while, but it then crossed over to the deep channel above the green croy on the right bank. By this time, Bill had taken a hand in playing the fish and, as he was almost out of backing, I told him to throw the rod over the side when he ran out – as he did. The rod departed upstream. We then went ashore and manhandled the boat round the green croy on the right bank under the pylon wires. I rowed upstream for about 100 yards then across, looking for the rod, reel and line. I spotted it, Bill gaffed the line, recovered the rod and started playing the fish again. I rowed to quieter water on the far side and took the rod over. Three other companions then arrived to watch the fish going up and down the deep channel after swimming round the boat but never within gaffing range.

At about 4 pm, William Wilson, who was managing Loch Leven, arrived from fishing elsewhere and took the oars, Bill being grateful to leave the boat, and another fishing companion, called Hugh, jumped in with some cigarettes, as I had long since run out. The fish took off upstream again and was soon 80 yards ahead of us, heading for the Breeches. William did well to keep up but, when we got there, it turned and ran downstream. We thought we might ambush him at the green croy but he kept going straight down to the Minister.

At about 5 pm we went ashore below the fence and tried to walk him but he would not come into the shallow water. As a last resort, William got the boat and went to the far side, where we would try again to drown him, but he would not stop swimming. We saw him quite clearly as he circled the boat – a perfect cock fish of immense depth – but at no time did he come close enough to gaff. I was trying again to lift him when the hooks came out. He had taken the Collie Dog and one of its double hooks was crushed, the other straightened. I cannot say that I was upset because I was so exhausted, mentally and physically. The battle had lasted almost eight hours.

Looking back, it must appear that anyone who plays a fish for that length of time must be a fool but I played it as hard as I dared. I had previously caught a 43-pounder without comparable difficulty. I saw the fish on about 10 occasions and he was a cock salmon of immense girth though probably less than 4 feet long. It was an experience I would not have missed, but wish never to repeat. I wrote my recollection of the struggle in the Beauly Estate office for the records there immediately afterwards.

Michael was certainly determined to catch that fish if he could. I have thrown my rod into the water accidentally but have never heard of a rod being thrown in deliberately and twice at that! The 64-pound record salmon caught on the Tay in 1922 was 4 feet 6 inches long but was not of enormous girth. So Michael's monster, which was a so-called 'portmanteau' fish because it was so deep and wide, could have exceeded that weight. Further, it would have been caught on a fly while the 64-pounder was caught on a bait being harled. However, I doubt whether Michael could have claimed a record, because his companion had shared the playing when he had needed a rest.

I feel even more deeply for a friend of mine, Sir Seton Wills, following his experience on the Varzina River in the Kola Peninsula, near Murmansk, which has been opened for salmon fishing. In June 1993, after a gruelling walk alone in dreadful weather to a tidal stretch allotted to him, he hooked a huge fish on a barbless Number 6 Mickey Finn fly. It tore up and down the big, strong river so energetically that it tired itself out in less than an hour and Sir Seton was able to half-beach it in shallow water. Having no spring-balance with him he was unable to weigh it but he did measure its length as 56 inches, with a girth to match – 2 inches longer than the Tay record. Sadly, he had no camera with him, either. The rules required him to return the fish and, in any case, the prospect of lugging such a monster back to camp was too much. After holding it in the water until it had recovered, he watched the biggest salmon he is ever likely to catch, especially on fly, swim away unweighed and unwitnessed by anyone else. Back at camp it was agreed that, with such dimensions, it must have weighed more than 60 pounds and could have been 70 or even more, although Sir Seton is too modest to make any claims himself.

The Tay monster, another fresh-run cock fish, was caught by a woman, Miss Georgina Ballantine, who killed it in just over two hours. As other huge salmon have fallen to female anglers, I wonder if one of us might have landed Michael Smith's. I am not suggesting that any woman would have been more expert at playing it or that we could have withstood such a strain, but we do seem to have more luck – so much so that my husband calls us the Unfair Sex so far as fishing goes.

Chapter 2

The Unfair Sex?

There is a theory, recently the subject of much publicity, that women tend to catch bigger fish than men do because their sexual scents – called pheromones when they get into the air – waft into the water and encourage the fish to bite. There is no doubt that fish have an astonishing sense of smell, salmon in particular being able to sense their way back to the river and often to the creek in which they were hatched. Experiments have shown that salmon become alarmed if a bear puts its paw in the water many yards upstream because they can detect the scent. Nevertheless, my husband, who is a former biologist, insists that the theory is rubbish, being based only on the fact that a few of the biggest salmon and trout caught in Britain have fallen to women. How, he asks, do the pheromones waft into the water from a woman encased up to the armpits in chest waders? And why should they attract only the big fish and fish of both sexes? He thinks that women owe their success either to luck or to being more patient, especially when fishing a salmon pool. He has his own theory that the more disabled a bait or a fly looks, the more likely a fish is to take it because it is instinctively attracted by prey that looks like easy meat. And a woman, fishing a pool down slowly and taking more time than a man before recasting, gives the lure more chance of looking helpless. Nevertheless, I get ribbed when I catch a big fish, with cries from the men of 'Waft some of them over my pool!'

A few of my friends are inclined to think there might be something in the idea since I broke two records on our Kennet trout fishing with an 8½-pound brownie on a dry fly and a 10½-pound rainbow on a nymph. On both occasions I was fortunate that my husband was near with his big net for neither would have fitted into mine. At least my pheromones were keeping him close by! Sadly, as he was quick to point out, both fish were female and presumably my sexual scents should only attract cock fish for, as he can testify, there is nothing gay about me. So what does that imply?

When questioned about the theory, one successful lady angler, said that she would not waste her pheromones on a fish. I would, especially if it was a salmon. As for my husband, he says that I gaffed him. Still, I think it worthwhile to put on record a few more monsters caught by what, if the theory is correct, 'would be called the unfair sex. Take, for instance, the experience of Lilla Rowcliffe.

I just could not understand how people could like fishing. Nevertheless, when friends asked me to fish on the River Shin in the far north of Scotland, with the promise of being shown how to do it, I accepted. I began to enjoy casting and when, with their help, I caught two salmon, I became determined to improve my skill. Soon after that I was asked by my cousin to join a party on the Delagyle beat of the Spey as someone had suddenly fallen out. On a foggy September day I journeyed north with tackle which I would now consider miserably inadequate. The following morning, when everyone was selecting from loads of tackle, the ghillie looked at mine and clearly sensed that I was inexperienced. As the river was high it was decided that we would all spin, something I had done only twice before. A cousin lent me a spinning reel and a green and yellow Devon Minnow. I tied it on, not being sure of the knot, but I was told that that it looked all right.

By the time I was ready the other rods were fishing so I walked upstream to a corner where the bank had been boarded up with wood. Suddenly, in the deep water on the corner, I saw a fish 'head and tail'. I was delighted that it was so near because I knew that even I could cast that far. I remembered being told that a head and tail riser was often a taking fish and cast, full of hope. At the fifth throw I felt a mighty pull and shouted, 'I've got a fish!' My cousin's response could have been predicted – 'Are you sure you're not on the bottom?' I did not answer.

As the fish seemed to be pulling me along I began to worry about the knot and decided that I had to play the fish gently. The ghillie, who had appeared, urged me to play it harder but shrugged and went away as I clearly had no intention of doing so. An hour later I was still playing it, having been taken down to the fishing hut. As it stormed across the river I realised how big it was and became more nervous than ever. After rushing about the pool it suddenly gave up and as I reeled in, my cousin came with the net. As I was up on the bank I could hardly see what was going on and heard the ghillie shout, 'Bloody Hell! We can't get it in the net.' Fortunately he was able to grab the tail when its head and shoulders were in the net. When I saw it I could not believe my eyes. It was 4 feet 6 inches long and weighed 45 pounds 6 ounces.

'What a big fish!' I thought. 'I ought to take up fishing seriously.' I was well and truly hooked, but I have never caught a really big salmon since.

The big fish story told to me by Annie Griggs (now Stewart) is even more extraordinary on two counts. When quite young, in late August 1958, just when dusk was falling, she made her first-ever cast with a salmon rod in the Aberdeenshire Dee at Aboyne, in the company of a gentleman called Fraser Bird. He told her where to put the fly into a fairly easy stream, and it was immediately taken by a 25-pound salmon which, with her friend's skilled assistance, she landed. It was quite an achievement to catch such a fish with her first cast but what, was even more remarkable in my view, was that she never fished again. So she caught her salmon on her one and only cast!

There are various ways of impressing a new husband and mine was to catch a salmon on the first day I ever tried for one. My dear friend Connie Ward, who had recently married the owner of the splendid Kinnaird stretch of the Tay, not only went two better but did it in remarkable style.

Early in September 1975 my new husband, Reggie, and I arrived at Kinnaird to get the house ready to receive the usual fishing house-guests who stayed, in rotation, until the season ended in mid-October. Everything was soon in order and, although I knew that I would not have much spare time, I was looking forward to the odd hour of fishing myself. Unfortunately, things began to go wrong, especially when the head gardener died of a heart attack during the first week. Fresh flowers in every room had always been a feature of the large house and, determined to impress upon Reggie that I could cope with any eventuality, I took on the flowers, which had never been one of my talents. This made such inroads into my time that I was unable to get to the river except to organise and oversee the picnic which we always held in the main fishing hut on the staff's free day.

On the final day of the season, however, with the house about to close, I ventured down to the Ash Tree pool and boarded the boat rowed by two ghillies. Armed with my new spinning rod, I began to fish, hooking an 11-pound salmon on the fifth cast. Encouraged by the ghillies to repeat the performance, I managed to land a 15-pounder. By this time my husband had arrived on the bank to see how I was faring and to escort me back to lunch. Pointing at his watch he obviously wanted me to stop, but the ghillies urged, 'Have a last cast, Madam.' So I did. It was the beginning of a monumental tussle which ended in the landing of a 31-pound fish, easily the largest salmon caught during the house party and setting the seal on the new marriage. As I was to learn later, most regular salmon fishers never have the luck to catch a 30-pounder.

Were Connie's pheromones responsible? The same question could be asked about the even bigger fish caught in the same pool by my glamorous friend and neighbour Sue Gilmour, who is remembered by many, to this day, for her appearance at Kinnaird in 'hot pants' during their brief popularity.

> I was fishing the Ash Tree, the most famous pool on the Kinnaird beat of the Tay, being rowed in that deep, swirling water in a boat accompanied by two ghillies. After the fly had failed I was casting a spinner when I encountered something rock solid and announced that, sadly, I was stuck on the bottom. Both ghillies assured me that it was impossible to foul the bottom there and they were right. 'Bonny Scotland', as they call the bottom, began to move, slowly but steadily, and there was no doubt that I was into a big fish. The time was about 12.45 and I was rowed ashore to play the fish from the bank.
>
> I had not been there long, with the fish making all the decisions, when my host, the late Reggie Ward, appeared. His delight at seeing me into a big salmon quickly turned to concern as the minutes ticked by with little impact on the fish. He soon began to worry that I might hold up the lunch, for which the other guests were already assembling back at the big house. With an admonition to get on with it he left me to join his other guests.
>
> I was rather late for lunch but we eventually beached the salmon which weighed 32 pounds. These days many – probably most – anglers fish all their lives and never encounter a 30-pounder and I was not going to lose mine. The ghillies agreed with my attitude but I was assured by the older of them that in the days of Reggie Ward's father, a stickler for protocol, they would have been instructed to cut the line, however big the fish, rather than permit their charge to be late at the lunch table.

As with Connie Ward's fish, I doubt whether pheromones had anything to do with Sue's, attractive though both of them are. After all, there were two men very close in each case and presumably they have pheromones too. The same applies to the record 64-pound salmon caught by Miss Ballantyne on the Glendevline beat of the Tay in 1922. She and her great fish are put forward as evidence for the female pheromone theory, but she was harling in a boat with her father, the head ghillie, and did not even have hold of the rod when the great fish took. I put a bait over the same lie several times in 1990, hoping that my pheromones might repeat the process, but with no result.

I must say it would make people think if the record was broken again by a woman! That it will be broken one day I have no doubt. Fish up to 70 pounds have been taken in the Tay nets and, occasionally,

Granny wields the brolly

dead fish are found which almost certainly would have exceeded the record when alive. Jim Tritton, one of the Kinnaird ghillies, told me about a huge fish which was found dead quite recently by a Tayside farmer. Its carcase was so big that he felt he should bury it. When the water authorities eventually heard about it however, they asked him to exhume it. Though much decomposed, its remains weighed more than 50 pounds and the opinion was that it could have scaled 70 when alive. So every time I fish the Tay I live in hope.

Sue Gilmour's great fish was much admired, which was more than could be said for a pike almost as big caught by the late Bobby St John Cooper, the cartoonist who invented Mr Cube for the Tate and Lyle sugar company. He was a keen but careless fisherman who rarely bothered to inspect his tackle from one expedition to the next. Spinning a lake one day, he hooked a huge pike which repeatedly took out his line beyond the point where there was an untidy knot in it. He grimaced every time the knot appeared but the line held and he duly grassed a superb hen pike weighing over 30 pounds. It was normal, in those days, to dispatch such a fish and the pike was laid on the bank when two middle-aged ladies strolled by.

'Oh look, he's caught a fish,' one of them remarked without stopping. 'So he has,' replied the other as both walked on without a backward glance.

However, I think that the true story supplied by Gerald Benney, goldsmith and silversmith to the Queen, the Queen Mother and other members of the Royal Family takes the prize for feminine nonchalance.

> Four of us had been fishing all day for salmon on the Nursling beat of the Test without success. As twilight crept up on us, Granny was standing silently on a low bridge, leaning on her furled umbrella, by a pool called the Drawing Room because it is so easy to fish. Suddenly a large salmon leapt clear out of the water and, like lightning, the brolly struck and down came the fish. It weighed 10 pounds and was the only one accounted for that day. I am afraid that we kept it.

Further evidence that, on the river at least, one should never under-estimate the power of a woman was provided by Miss Effie Barker of Stanlake Park near Twyford, a fishing guest on the stretch of the Kennet where I fish. Now 80, she was Master of the Garth Hunt for 28 years and invented the Nab, the English version of the McNab – the feat of killing a stag, a grouse and a salmon on the same day, which is rather difficult south of the border. Her version was to hunt and kill a fox, shoot a partridge and catch a trout. Then for good measure she played and won two sets of tennis, played a game of squash, drove herself to London and arrived at a friend's house properly dressed for dinner.

Whatever the truth of the pheromone theory, I for one will just go on fishing as before, enjoying what sport comes my way and keeping my eyes open to all the wonderful things that are there to be seen in the quiet of the riverside.

Chapter 3

Nature Watch

No other sport brings its participants into such close contact with the natural world as fishing does. Over the years it has opened my eyes to so much of which I was previously unaware, even though I had been brought up in the Norfolk countryside when it was much more unspoiled than it is today. In addition, others have told me about their observations on the riverside. Some of their stories are of the unexpected, even the mysterious, others are of nature's rapacity, while most are of simple, sometimes earthy, delights.

Typical of the first category is the story – a literal tail of the unexpected – supplied by Don Macer-Wright of Dean Hall at Little Dean, in Gloucestershire, whose company I enjoyed when he looked after the stretch of the Kennet where I fish.

> I was recently on the banks of the Wye at a favourite and hidden spot where the river winds along the edge of the Forest of Dean, and I was privy to an extraordinary collection of natural events which, in the southern Britain of the 1990s, seem totally implausible. While contemplating the scene before me and wondering where else one could hear the calls of ravens, buzzards and a peregrine falcon all at the same time, I suddenly noticed a most peculiar tail. Below me, in the water, a tangle of willow caused a slack and, at the head of it, I could see a motionless tail pointing upstream in the oddest position, facing the current. Suddenly, a large old fallow buck intruded itself into my vision and, to my astonishment, disturbed an otter, which slid down the bank into the tangled willow. At that moment the tail I had spotted shot out of the cover to reveal a huge pike, over 25 pounds, with a half-swallowed fish in its jaws. The pike made an enormous swirl and disturbed the buck which, sensing me then, made off into the woodland thicket. The whole experience had happened in the space of a few seconds.

The kingfisher figures frequently in the stories I have come across, but nowhere more delightfully than in that provided by Mr George Willis, a builder from Feltham.

I had been carp fishing all night, using two rods in Bedfont Lake, a former gravel pit in Middlesex. As usual I was sitting on a bed-chair under a big umbrella. When dawn broke the morning was fine. I poured a cup of coffee and was rolling a cigarette when a kingfisher came and settled on the right-hand rod. This had happened to me several times before in my long hours of carp fishing. I froze to watch it as it dived from the rod and caught a small fish which it killed by dashing it against the carbon-fibre rod before swallowing it. It did this twice more and then became interested in the line, which was hanging limp. It reached over, took the line in its beak and set off the little bite-alarm. This startled it but did not make it fly. I noticed later that its beak had been so sharp that it had kinked the nylon line.

The bird then flew off about 15 yards and settled on a piece of concrete about 5 feet above the water, so I continued to watch its antics. It dived and flew back with another fish which it killed, but this time instead of swallowing it the bird shuffled to the edge of the concrete and dropped it into the water. The fish sank and the kingfisher dived again to retrieve it. Knowing that it was already dead, the bird did not dash the fish against the concrete but immediately dropped it back into the water. This performance was repeated five or six times and I was left in no doubt that either the kingfisher was getting in some diving practice or was simply enjoying itself playing with the fish. I did not catch a carp, so the bird provided the highlight of the outing.

The brief experience recorded in the diary of Colin Farnell, a fellow member of my trout syndicate, was probably rarer in ornithological terms.

In June 1973, while I was standing very still holding my split cane fly rod waiting for a fish to rise, a reed bunting perched on the end of it.

Steven Penney, head river keeper to the Duke of Wellington at Stratfield Saye, witnessed some surprising bird behaviour on a rather larger scale.

While fishing the Kennet with a friend we both saw a heron fly off with a full-grown tufted duck in its bill. Astonished that it could carry such a load, we did all we could to frighten it into dropping the duck, which was still alive because we could see its legs moving, but we had no success. It was November so the heron was not taking it back to a nest to feed its young and was, I suppose, taking it to feed off it itself.

While herons regularly take ducklings nobody I have met has

seen or heard anything like this behaviour. However, I have seen two ducks, one of them a full-grown mallard, with heron stab wounds.

As an example of excessively greedy predation, the story given to me by Andrew Hicks would be hard to better.

> I was beside the lake at Elnham House in Norfolk, talking to friends, when we noticed a fully grown mute swan with its head under water and its tail up as though feeding on the bottom. After a while one of us remarked that the swan's head had been submerged for rather a long time. When it remained tail-up for several more minutes, we went to investigate. We managed to pull it into the side without a struggle and were astonished to find that its head was firmly clamped inside the jaws of a large pike. Both creatures were dead. The swan had drowned because the pike, which weighed 12 pounds, had been too heavy for it to heave out of the water. The pike had been unable to breathe because the swan's head and beak were so far down its throat that its gills could not function, while its backward-pointing teeth had made regurgitation impossible.
>
> Clearly, the pike had seen the head and neck of the swan as manageable prey but the body of what is the world's heaviest flying bird had been too much for it.

The experience on the Aberdeenshire Dee of Richard Warrin, who is well known in the golfing world, was rather more frightening – at least for a moment or two.

> On Commonty beat, on a very hot summer's day in August 1990, I went down to say hello to the ghillie and there was a man fishing whom I did not know. I shouted 'Is Dan about?' He could not hear me because of the noise of the river and started to come out, saying 'I'm tired, I'm coming out anyway.' We stood on the bank chatting when suddenly I saw the man's eyes widen with astonishment. There was a huge hawk or falcon coming straight for my face. I was quite terrified and ducked as it hit me on the shoulder. The bird then landed on a boulder about 20 yards away and we saw that it had a leather thong on its legs. Obviously, it was a tamed hawk which had been trying to land on my shoulder. We never did catch it.

Steven Penney's, experience, again on a smaller scale, was nevertheless extraordinary.

> While walking up the river Loddon at Stratfield Saye, for which I am responsible, I was watching a small water vole swimming

14

An abundance of wildlife

across the stream when a kestrel swooped down on it and took it. Again, nobody I have spoken to about this has ever seen the like.

Another piscatorial Penney, Bruce of that name, who is a salmon fishing friend of mine, had a closer encounter with a bird of no mean size.

I hooked a swan with a salmon fly, in the web of one foot, and fully expected to be broken when the bird managed to get almost airborne. Instead it crashed down and seemed quite shattered as I reeled it in on my 15-foot carbon-fibre rod. I was using only a 15-pound breaking strain cast but the huge bird could not break it. I managed to get hold of it and released it.

Pursuing the ornithological theme, the story supplied to me by Nevile Clifford-Jones, a retired Surrey businessman, is surely unique.

Having taken ponies up the escarpment from the Drakensberg in South Africa to a remote part of Lesotho in October 1975, I was fly fishing in rivers which are seldom visited. I was fortunate enough to catch a rainbow trout weighing 7 pounds 10 ounces which, according to the natives, was of such unusual size that I decided to have it mounted. Although it was beginning to smell by the time I got it to Durban, I delivered it to an Indian taxidermist who mounted it on a board and, one year later, it arrived at my home in Surrey. It lived in the house for several years but when it began to fall to pieces it was banished to a hut by the bathing pool where it deteriorated further. Nevertheless, it was to serve a useful, if unusual, purpose.

In the spring of 1984 a pair of spotted flycatchers decided that it was a perfect nesting site. They built on – and partly in – it, and successfully reared their brood of four. The flycatchers, which could well have migrated from South Africa, had found a home on a South African fish!

While Roy Bush, a coarse fish specialist from Richmond, Surrey, is not particularly allergic to snakes, as I am, he was not too pleased when he parted a bankside bush by the River Kennet, thinking a slight commotion under it might be caused by a carp, and found it was a snake, which hissed at his face. The snake swam to the opposite bank but then returned, by which time a passer-by had stopped to watch it. He assured Mr Bush that it was an adder, which could easily have bitten him. It seems more likely that it was a harmless grass-snake but I can confirm that, close by, there is a house which, to deter trespassers, used to display a large notice 'Alive with adders!'

There is no doubt about the authenticity of the creature witnessed by Ron Benjamin, the keen match angler, who owns the Field and Stream sports shop in Newbury and supplied this first-hand account.

George Blake looked at his watch. There was not long to
go before the final whistle which would end the club fishing
competition. His float suddenly dipped and he played what felt
like a good-sized eel, which he guided into the landing net. As he
struggled to withdraw the hook, his catch twisted and turned in
his hands, as eels do, and as the hook came free it slid out of his
hands into the grass. Finding it after a few moments, he grasped it
and flung it into the keep-net as the match ended.

'Let's see what you've got, George,' the scalesman said affably,
as he arrived at the peg. George dragged the keep-net out of the
water and poured the fish into the weigh-net when suddenly there
was a mad rush away from the water. George was left looking at
an open weigh-net where, in the middle of the flapping roach and
dace, lay a 2-foot long adder.

It was a different but equally unwelcome creature which intruded into
the sport of David Roache of Northend, near Banbury.

When I was about 12 years old I had induced my father, who was
not a keen fisherman, to take me in his car to the Oxford Canal on
a bitterly cold day. It was so cold, in fact, that the canal was frozen
over save for a patch by a bridge where we could both get our
floats in. After about three hours without a bite, my father decided
to eat a small pork pie which he had brought as part of his lunch.
He had just bitten into it when his float went down. I drew his
attention to it but he struck too late and the fish, whatever it was,
escaped. So did his pork pie. We turned to see a huge, furry rat
making off with it.

There are few more acute observers of nature than Shirley Deterding,
the noted Norfolk sportswoman and artist, and few who have fished
in so many parts of the world. The tale she told me was also of fur.

It is not only the fish that make the Michaels River so exciting
to those who love the Labrador wilderness. Sitting in a corner of
sunshine with my back to some bushes, I was suddenly aware of
a flash of black fur passing over my legs. I went on reading and
a few seconds later it happened again. I watched and the small
creature reappeared to glare at me with sharp bright eyes. It was a
lemming and I was sitting on the main run to her home while she
was collecting food for her family.

On another peaceful, warm afternoon I was sitting painting the
pool I had just fished with moderate success when I heard a cough.
The hairs on the back of my neck bristled, for I knew there was
not another living soul within 5 miles. There were two wolves
standing on the edge of the water wondering what I was doing in

their territory. Ignoring me, they finished lapping and trotted off the way they had come.

The otter is the furry creature most likely to feature in a fish tale and two more have come my way to add to those recorded in my first volume. While I was fishing the Little Blackhall beat of the Dee recently, the ghillie there, Norman Sinclair, supplied this anecdote.

In the early spring of 1990, a young man called Coleman was a member of a fishing party which had been flogging the Little Blackhall beat for a week with no success, mainly because the river had been up and down daily so that the salmon never settled. After packing up on the final day Coleman went to have a last look at the gauge at the Seat pool to see what the river was doing. As he did so he saw a commotion in the slack water by the gauge and realised that it was an otter which had quite a nice salmon by the tail and was trying to land it. He ran the 40 yards or so to the ghillie's hut, seized a net and hared back to the pool. The otter was still struggling with the fish and as Coleman approached it with the net it dropped its prey which was duly netted. It was nice fresh fish weighing $8^1/2$ pounds. So Mr Coleman did not go home without a fish.

What is extraordinary is that someone fishing the opposite bank of Blackhall that same week, Richard Warrin, whom I have already mentioned, gave me an almost identical tale.

While fishing Mr Stewart Spence's beat, Commonty, on the Aberdeenshire Dee, not far upstream from Blackhall, my son, Steve, who was 38 at the time and on his first salmon-fishing trip, was walking up the beat with Dan Dowell, the ghillie. Steve spotted a salmon behaving in a strange way on the surface as though jumping across the water and the ghillie then saw that it was in the jaws of an otter which eventually dragged it on to the bank about 100 yards away. Fortunately, this was the bank from which we were fishing.

Dowell told my son to get down there quickly and frighten the otter, which he did. So the otter provided my son with his first salmon, a 12-pounder.

I do not imagine that there are many otters left on the Wye. Sadly, their environmental niche there has been filled by the unloveable mink, the progeny of ranched stock probably released by the animal rights fanatics who have done such damage to wild animals through their ignorance and stupidity. As mink kill salmon as well as waterfowl, they get little quarter from ghillies, as George Johnson, a retired head ghillie from the Wye recounted to me when I was fishing there.

18

On the Cadora beat, where I was employed, I noticed some ducks quacking loudly in the gin-clear water and saw a mink catching eels on the bottom underneath them. I picked up my gun, which I always had in the boat with me in case of such opportunities, and shot at the mink which had emerged on to the bank with an eel in its mouth. To my annoyance, I missed but the mink dropped the eel before making off. Not to be outdone, and realising that the mink must be hungry, I picked up the eel, tied it to a long string and waited for the mink to return. Sure enough it did and I then dragged the eel along the bank with the mink following it until the animal was within easy range. I did not miss it a second time.

There was no mystery as to how that eel found itself on the bank but Steven Penney remains puzzled to this day about a bankside trout.

On a very foggy morning in November I was walking up the stretch of the River Loddon at Stratfield Saye for which I am responsible, and spotted quite a large trout lying on the bank. It was dead but had no mark on it and was steaming – something I had never seen a fish do before. When I felt it it was quite warm and I have never been able to figure out why. The likeliest explanation is that a heron had pouched it and then disgorged it, perhaps when it heard me approaching through the fog. However, there was not a mark on the fish.

My husband, Harry Chapman Pincher, remains equally mystified by a similar experience.

While I was walking my chocolate Labrador dog, Dido, on Hungerford Common she stopped to inspect something in the grass which, in view of her interest, seemed likely to be the remains of a rabbit. I ran over to stop her eating it and was amazed to find her staring at a large grayling, certainly in excess of a pound weight. I examined the fish and it was fresh.
    We were at least a quarter of a mile from the river Kennet, from which the fish had presumably been taken. A human source seemed most unlikely so I assumed that it had been taken there by a heron to eat at leisure and the bird had been frightened off before we arrived. Alternatively, it might have been taken by a mink, but there was no mark on it.

The Hon. Charles Hill-Trevor of Chirk, in Clwyd, supplied a further memorable mink saga.

A burly, red-faced hill stalker, who was semi-retired through age, occasionally served as a ghillie for fishing guests on my family's estate in Argyllshire and, while doing so, noticed a commotion

19

among the salmon at the head of the pool which was being fished. He spotted the cause as he saw a mink emerge and, having heard about their ravages, though never having seen one before, determined to dispose of the nuisance if he could. Having preened itself on a rock, the mink slithered on to a path in the heather which led towards the bottom of the pool. Suddenly, the VIP fishing guest found himself pinned to the heather while the ghillie, using all his stalking skills made himself invisible and grasped the landing net. By that time the mink had taken to the water and was swimming down close to the bank. Stalking it with great skill, the ghillie extended the net into its path and netted the animal, quickly knocking it on the head with his priest. The angler, who had not seen the mink and for a few moments thought the ghillie had gone mad, regaled the other guests that evening with the story which, he thought, was even more memorable than catching a salmon.

In *Fish Tales* I was able to include several stories of anglers who had hooked wild creatures other than fish and a few more have been volunteered for this volume. Penny Radcliffe, a member of our trout-fishing club, told me that, while wading the Naver, a salmon angler's fly was very solidly taken and after a brief struggle he was amazed to see his catch rise out of the water and fly over his head, landing some 20 yards behind him in the heather. Armed with his priest, the angler traced his line to find, at the end of it, a very lively cormorant.

Sir Denis Mountain, who owns the wonderful Delfur beat of the Spey, related a similar experience. A man was fishing the Colley pool of his beat in the spring and his bait was taken by a razorbill, which was played, landed and released.

The unexpected ornithological encounter of my stepson, Michael Chapman Pincher, was aerial rather than aquatic, as he has vividly recorded.

We took Jerry on as a deck hand in Puerto Rico. He had been a lance corporal in Northern Ireland and was now a boat bum. From the stories he told as we sailed the Spanish Main towards Panama it was a good career move and, more than once, he proved to be the right man to have aboard when moving in waters where pirates still ply their trade. Far from the 'Troubles' nothing gave Jerry more pleasure than fishing and he was a natural – so natural, in fact, that the only thing that roused him from sleep was when the line screamed from the reel on the rod locked on the stern rail. As soon as our trolled bait was struck he was up and at it, sometimes stark naked, playing whatever Neptune had provided. Every day he would land fat bluefin tuna or a dorado the size of a child. Jerry was expert at getting me to steer the 8-ton ketch close to any piece of flotsam that might be offering shade to the delicious dorado, and then my job was to hang lively over the edge of the boat, gaff the catch clean behind the dorsal fin and haul it aboard for us all to watch in fascination as the fish's fluorescent yellow and green livery changed through a rainbow of colours till it died a steely grey on the deck.

Slipping through the Panama Canal we reached the Pacific, where mating turtles floated past, and at dawn the sea was full of bottle-nosed dolphins hunting the tuna beneath our hull. Mexico saw us struck down by Montezuma's Revenge and we only started fishing again as we set sail from the tip of Baja California bound for Vancouver. Early one morning, with wisps of autumn fog in the air, the reel screamed its alarm. In a second Jerry and I were on deck but the rod was not bent. We scoured the sea and then the sky. Above us, lumbering like a pterodactyl, was a pelican with our bait inside its bill. Jerry started to play her to the dismay of the Captain's daughters who were happy to see fish slaughtered for the table but angry to see a bird as our quarry. Soon the exhausted bird was floundering in the water and I was quickly over the side to try to land it. Far from being thankful that a blond, agile youth was coming to its rescue, the bird went on the attack. It was the size of a swan with a beak as sharp as Saladin's scimitar.

Fortunately, Jerry had taught me some of the tactics he had learned on the streets of Londonderry and soon I had the bird subdued and was back on deck with it. I extracted the hook and let it go but it just sat there while the girls proceeded to feed it with the rest of our bait. At sundown we moved into US waters with the pelican still sitting on the poop deck. By morning our illegal immigrant had gone and I went off for a scoop to clear the deck of its substantial parting gift.

My friend, James Klootwijk, a former Chairman of Shell and a former President of the Flyfishers' Club, was so impressed by his unexpected contact with a bird that he stopped fishing for a while to contemplate its significance in the grand pattern of nature.

I was trolling along the shore of Loch Tay, alone in a motor boat, with four rods out, one of them with an old-fashioned, feathery fly as a lure. I was not paying much attention to the water when I heard one of the reels starting to screech. As quickly as I could I stopped the engine and wound in the other three lines expecting a fight with a salmon. Instead I found that my remaining line was distinctly airborne – in fact, the lure was quite high in the air attached to a large gull which was doing its best to escape. I reeled in as quickly as possible to release the bird, fearing that I might have to kill it if it had swallowed the lure, and while I was doing so it was viciously attacked by several other gulls attracted by its struggles. They behaved in what we would describe as an incredibly cruel way while the hapless bird tried to defend itself. Here was one of their kind in terrible trouble and all that they could do was to try and kill it in the hope of an easy meal.

Fortunately, when I finally hauled the bird in I found it was just hooked in the web of one of its feet and seemed to have escaped the other gulls' savage beaks. As I tried to release the hook with minimum damage it bit me but eventually flew away with the others no longer in pursuit. It was only when they thought that it could not defend itself that they attacked it. Here, I thought, was Darwinism in action – the survival of the fittest. Not only would the handicapped creature make a meal for the healthy but it would be prevented from breeding, which might benefit the species as a whole.

The experience of my neighbour, Sir John Bowman, was more in line with the previous anecdotes I had collected, but was probably unique in one respect.

For all I know there may be many instances when a swallow, a swift or even a bat has hitched itself to an artificial fly as it moves through the air while being cast, mistaking it for a real one. It must surely be rare, however, for it to happen twice to the same angler as it has to me, especially as both events occurred on the same water – the Craven stretch of the River Kennet.

On the first occasion, a bright sunny day in June, the unfortunate creature was a swift. I cast at a rising fish with a dry fly and the bird caught it in mid-air. I did not know what had happened until I realised that the line was being tugged around in the air. I managed to ground the bird on the bank from which, being a swift with its weak legs, it could not easily take off again, and extracted the fly from its beak without much injury. It then flew off from my open hand.

In the second instance, I was lingering on the river until it was almost dark, perhaps because it the very last day of the season, 30 September. Again I did not see the strike but realised that something odd had happened and then discovered that my fly had been taken by a small bat. Sadly, I was unable to extract the fly without serious injury and the Craven bat population had to be reduced by one.

The unusual catch made by Nick Faldo, who wields a rod as well as a golf club, was somewhat larger. He was fishing the Tufton beat of the Test as a guest of John Fowles, and had no success for about an hour. A curious Friesian cow came and stood some 20 yards behind him, and when Faldo extended his cast to cover a trout on the far side of the river his fly made contact with the beast's rump. The cow took off, taking out line and backing, with Faldo and the ghillie chasing after it.

Eventually it was cornered, the line wound in and the fly recovered. As the barb was well embedded it removed a tiny piece of skin and a tuft of hair from the cow's hide when it was removed. At the ghillie's suggestion, Faldo kept the additional 'hackle' on for luck and subsequently caught several trout with it. Has cow hackle been used before, or did Nick invent something?

The creature hooked – deliberately – by Colin Farnell was somewhat smaller.

> Being a lover of river banks, I do not regard water voles, which tunnel holes in them and can cause parts to collapse when there are a lot of them, as nice creatures. So one day, when I was standing by the water's edge and saw a vole swimming towards me from the other side, I cast my fly at it, hooked it, landed it and dispatched it. I even recorded it in my fishing diary – caught on a Size 14 gold-ribbed Hare's Ear!
>
> A couple of years later I repeated the process on the Kennet but with a Pheasant Tail nymph.

For my part, the vole is an essential part of the river scene and, although they have often deluded me into believing that a fish was on the move, I enjoy their company. I also suspect that they play some useful part in the natural balance of the river. That usually turns out to be true of most of the creatures we may regard as a nuisance, as David Gardiner, who lives close by in Berkshire, confirmed.

> I first took the Moorbridge beat of the Lambourn, just below Boxford, in 1968 and had it for the next 13 seasons. There was 1/2 mile of fishing and we had a mini-syndicate of three friends, organising our own stocking and water-keeping. The Lambourn is a little river but with great character, growing small trout, never more than 1 1/2 pounds but very sporting. If a bigger trout is caught it is usually a Kennet fish which has come upstream. During my time I never stocked it with fish of more than 3/4 pound which still had growing capacity. Because the river is shallow, fast flowing and rather cold, to have put in 2- or 3-pound fish would have been to condemn them to slow death by starvation.
>
> During our first season it became apparent that there was a

very large number of grayling on the beat which had to compete with the trout for the limited food. So in April, before the second season started, I arranged for the local angling club to electric fish the beat with the safer DC stunner and take away the grayling for their own water. They took 222 grayling of up to 1½ pounds and, as some of them were taken on the main trout-spawning beds, I knocked a few on the head and opened up their stomachs. To my surprise I found trout fry inside them, some with the egg sac still attached. So, I thought, we were doing more than just removing food competitors.

Encouraged by this operation, I induced the angling club to repeat it in the ensuing spring, when they took 320 grayling, and in the spring after that when they removed about 400. There was a significant change in the trout fishing but not one that we enjoyed. During our first season we had caught several trout over 1 pound and set ourselves a lower limit of ½ pound. But during the three seasons when we had removed the grayling we caught only one-pounder. There was also a big increase in the number of small trout of 5 or 6 ounces, so much so that they were a nuisance. This led me to two tentative conclusions. First, the larger trout, which appeared to be unharmed by the stunner, may have died a few days after being released. Secondly, the thinning out of the trout fry by the grayling had prevented over-population. Once the grayling were removed, there were too many and there was not enough food in the little river to let them grow to a decent size.

We therefore discontinued electric fishing and soon began to catch many 1-pounders and ceased to be troubled by small trout. There are times when nature can maintain its own balance better than we can.

While I know that everything has its place in nature, there are a few things I can do without and flies – other than those which attract the trout – and wasps are two of them. The grey biting flies are the worst but they can all be a nuisance as Ron Benjamin, the Newbury tackle dealer, discovered.

One Sunday, the club's tench trophy was due to be fished for on a small private lake near Faringdon, in Oxfordshire. Bob Spiers and I had never won the trophy so we decided to take special steps to remedy that. Bob was a butcher and, knowing that tench were attracted to ground-bait containing dried blood, we resolved to take a bucket of fresh pig's blood to the competition and mix it, on the bank, with dry breadcrumbs to form both hook-baits and ground-bait. With so much available we felt confident.

About 20 keen anglers assembled by the lake where, it was

known, the best swims were under the trees at the top of the lake. Unfortunately, when the draw was made, Bob and I did not pick places there but were next to each other in what was clearly going to be a very hot spot with no breath of wind.

At 10 am the whistle went for the start, but before that we had mixed our bait, which turned out to be much stickier than we had imagined so that not only our hands, but the cuffs of our sleeves and anything else we touched smelled of blood once we began throwing in the ground-bait. In no time we attracted every fly in the area, and soon they were pestering us in droves.

Pandemonium had also broken out at the top of the lake under the trees because one of the competitors, a little chap with a reputation for being 'jinxed', had drawn a place which happened to contain a wasps' nest. To avoid this he had had to move to a spot which was awkward for casting, and with his second attempt his line was entangled in a branch above him. His attempts to free it failed and after he had lost everything, including his float and the top joint of his rod, he decided to climb the tree armed with a hacksaw blade, much to the annoyance of his neighbours, who knew that tench are very wary of any disturbance.

Once up the tree he proceeded to cut the branch off and down it came into the water with a great splash, for which he was immediately disqualified. With nothing to lose, he waded into the water to recover the branch which was floating away and – yes, you have guessed it – while pulling it up the bank he disturbed the wasps' nest. Out they swarmed attacking everyone in sight. There was chaos all round and, as Bob and I had already withdrawn to escape the flies, the match was declared void and abandoned.

Many an angler has been harried off the river by that more vicious insect, the mosquito, which oddly seems to be most numerous, biggest and most vicious within the Arctic Circle. Several of my friends will not face the Ponoi River in Russia because of the 'mossies' which are so voracious that they seem to defeat every precaution. Shirley Deterding, who encounters them on her fishing trips to Labrador, has her own method for dealing with them, one which is hardly applicable on most rivers.

The mosquitoes in Labrador are twice the size and have twice the biting power of the ordinary variety. Each bite comes up twice. Some people wear heavy nets all the time but I find them too claustrophobic and it is impossible to paint in them. So my forehead and other parts which have to be bared from time to time end up looking like the Atlas Mountains.

Anti-bug sprays and lotions are not really effective and can cause havoc with your tackle. Some of them literally dissolve fishing lines and they are not too good on the flesh either. So before removing any clothes, if it gets too hot in the sun, I smoke a pipe to create a haze, but I usually seem to trap a dozen mosquitoes and black flies in my underwear and they go on biting there for the next hour or so. Fortunately, in the wilderness, modesty does not worry me too much and, on one occasion when the flies were especially pestilential, I shed all my clothes and jumped into the water for a swim.

Shirley's rather extreme recipe reminds me that I opened this chapter by saying that no other sport brings its participants into such close contact with the natural world as fishing does. Of course, what the angler sees or does not see depends on the intensity of his concentration on the task in hand. If this is excessive he can completely miss the unexpected, as Bill Rushmer, a well-known coarse fisherman of Ashford in Middlesex, records – with a touch of regret, I suspect.

I was fishing the Little Pond at Frensham in Surrey with a few friends very early one summer morning in 1987. We had arrived at about 4 am to try for some of the big tench there. I had not been fishing long, watching my waggler float with great intensity, when I was into a good fish and called for my net, which was a few yards away because I had moved a short distance on hooking the fish. Although I could hear my friends close by, nobody came to my assistance. All I could hear was a lot of clicking as though they were practising with the cameras which every coarse fishermen takes with him to photograph any specimen fish before returning it to the water. Eventually, I had to feel for the net myself and landed the tench, which was a beauty weighing 6 pounds 5 ounces. 'Thank you all very much,' I shouted scathingly as I photographed my fish. Again there was no response. By the time I had rebaited they were prepared to give me some attention and tell me what had been happening. While I had been busily engaged watching my float and then playing my fish an attractive young girl, who had preceded us to the lake for a pre-breakfast swim, had emerged from the water further down. She was stark naked and, as her car and clothes were on the other side of us, she simply strode past us, not a bit abashed, while my colleagues made the most of the situation with their cameras. She had been within 15 yards of my back and I never got a glimpse of her. In fact, I was not sure that I believed their story until, a few days later, I saw their photographs.

Chapter 4

Lucky Fishers

While skill and experience account for the greater part of an angler's success and satisfaction, there is no other sport where luck – of both kinds, good and bad – plays such a part. I have had my own run of both, especially with salmon, but so far the scales have been weighted on the side of good fortune. Like lucky generals, there are lucky fishers and my friends tell me I am one of them. Catching a good fish on my first day on a salmon river was the beginning and it has continued to an extent that caused my favourite ghillie, Bob Grant, to say 'There's never a dull moment when you're around!'

Mr Tony Richards, a surgeon at the Hampshire Clinic, near Basingstoke, seems similarly blessed.

One Easter weekend I was fishing the Towy, the Welsh salmon river where I had first learned to fish (with worms) at a very early age. The water was high and brown, and it had been a blank day for both myself and my friend, Emrys Lewis. It was raining so hard that it was with great difficulty that I had persuaded him to accompany me. At 5.30 we decided to call it a day but I remembered that, at the end of the previous season, the ghillie had shown me a lie at the top of the beat which we had not fished. As Emrys was to continue fishing, sadly without me, for several more days I thought that I should show him the lie and how to fish it.

I pointed out a bush on the other side and said, 'You stand here, throw the bait across the river at 45 degrees, aiming at that bush, wind gently for a bit and then let it swing slowly across the current.' As I stopped winding a 7½-pound sea-trout took the bait and was duly landed.

I then watched Emrys fish the lie but he was not doing it well. So I showed him the technique once more. My second cast produced a 9½-pound sea-trout.

On our way back downstream to the car we passed another lie we had not fished and I suggested that he should try it. He had always used fixed-spool reels but was keen to try the multiplier which I preferred. After a few poor casts which produced a bird's nest, he asked me to show him how to use it again. With the first cast I hooked a 20-pound salmon. Three fish in four casts after a blank day, and Emrys took them all – and my apologies – wonderfully well.

As with me, Tony Richards' luck goes way back to the time when he started.

I had always wanted a multiplying reel and when my uncle visited us from America he brought me a Shakespeare which, in those early days, did not have a slipping clutch. One day, standing up to my knees in the River Towy, trying to cast out a bunch of worms, I got a bird's nest and the bait landed no more than a couple of yards in front of me. Ten minutes elapsed while I sorted out the tangle and when I finally wound up the line a salmon had firmly hooked itself.

Even the greatest experts, like Richard Waddington, innovator of the salmon flies which bear his name, acknowledge their occasional debt to Lady Luck.

As a young man in my early twenties, in 1932, I was staying in a house party at Boughrood on the Upper Wye. On the Sunday morning old Sir Harmood Banner enquired whether anybody not going to church would like to go fishing. I thought that my immortal soul could look after itself for once and, together with one of the Johnston Houghtons, elected to try the river. Craven, the ghillie, fitted both of us out with spinning rods, identical casts, and with identically weighted spinning prawns. He then rowed us to the middle of the Home Catch, a famous pool, where we started casting, my companion from the bow and I from the stern. Craven kept the boat steady in the almost streamless pool.

Almost at once I was into a fish which, to the astonishment of all of us, failed to make the smallest effort to escape and was gaffed into the boat, still in mid-pool, within half a minute. A few casts later another fish took my prawn. Again it made no attempt to get away and was gaffed into the boat. By now Craven realised that there was a run of very fresh but very tired fish in the Home Catch. So we went on fishing and by midday I had hooked and landed six salmon, all in the 10–12-pound range, not one of which had played for more than a minute. Fishing with the same tackle my companion had never had a pull. At one moment we saw a fish which was following his prawn suddenly turn away and seize mine as it neared the boat.

I have never been able to find a satisfactory explanation for that extraordinary morning's fishing. Perhaps my bait was being fished faster or slower, or perhaps deeper. On the other hand, had it been just a matter of luck, the odds were the same as if I had left £1 on the roulette table to run on black and it had come up six times consecutively, when I would have collected £64. So the odds against my catching six fish while the other rod caught none were only 64 to one, not the thousands one tends to imagine.

Mark Farrer of Farrer and Co, the Queen's Solicitors, recalled one of his luckiest days in this manner.

For many years I had spent three or four weeks at Durness in north-west Sutherland, staying in some discomfort at a small hotel, known to this day as 'MacFawlty's' which enjoyed one of the finest views in Scotland and a truly exceptional variety of fishing on its day. The fishing was allocated on a rota system, the one certainty being that those with the first and second choice were almost guaranteed to catch the fish they were after, subject to the vagaries of the weather.

One Sunday evening in 1957 a strong gale was sweeping in from the south-west and the brownish tinge of the River Grudie told of a spate in the making – and we all lived for spates. At the top of the list, and therefore able to choose any part of the extensive fishings, were a doctor and a fruit farmer from Kent whom my brother and I cordially disliked. They had booked a boat on Loch Stack but in that weather they decided to cancel. It was then offered to us and in those days, since the death of my father, we could afford the extra cost only because a cheque for £13. 17s. 5d had unexpectedly arrived from Shell on the previous day.

On the following morning the gale was still blowing and we faced the possibility that we would not get afloat but have to spend the day in the boathouse. Our ghillie was going to be Donald, 45 years on the loch and still working in retirement. He was not large and his thick pebble glasses made one wonder how he coped with landing a fish, especially in the blasts of wind and torrents of rain. We assumed that it was too rough to dap but he firmly advised it, with conventional fly fishing in reserve only if that failed.

We were the first of four boats to cast off and head round the point into the great sea that was running down the loch. We played out two big, bushy flies down the wind and tried to control them amid the pitch and chop of the surface. Whenever we were able to get them to sail over the wave surface sea-trout came at them in meaningful fashion. There were seven of them in the boat at lunch as well as a good deal of surface water. After lunch, in waist-deep ancient heather which sheltered us, we put to sea again with no sign of an improvement in the weather. No sooner

Loch Stack in generous mood

had we turned into a new drift and loosed our dapping flies on to the waves than mine vanished in a quiet and deliberate fashion. The fish reacted by a long scything run upwind of the boat and a crashing leap at the end of it. There were several more fast runs but I was able to bring a sea-trout of 9½ pounds alongside. It had taken 20 minutes to play and we had drifted a long way down the loch, so Donald returned us to the head of the drift where my brother almost immediately took a sea-trout of 5½ pounds, the freshest and liveliest of the day.

In the afternoon we moved to a different area and almost immediately a rather brown salmon rolled out of the waves and took a large dry fly. I had it on for four or five dour minutes before it took its leave. Several more rose to the dap during our sweeps but did not get hold of the fly. After working down the shore without further success, we headed for home.

We were the last alongside and tied up at the end of the stone pier. Donald walked along peering into the other boats. All he could find was the odd finnock of about 2 pounds and not more than two of those per boat. His prowl excited the curiosity of the others, as did the boot of our car when we returned to the hotel. We had nine sea-trout weighing 41½ pounds while the two men who had turned the loch down had just two salmon.

Since then we have had salmon in abundance but we have never caught sea-trout like that. We had done it through taking a chance when it offered and trusting in the ghillie's advice when, to us, it seemed unlikely to succeed. We also owed it to that chance cheque from Shell, and shares in that company still form the backbone of my investment portfolio.

My husband reckons that every salmon take ultimately depends on the luck of putting the lure in front of a fish at the time when it is in the mood to have a go at it, which may be fleeting. Sometimes one does not really deserve it, as he recalled.

I was standing on the left bank of the River Spey, on the famous Delfur beat, while the ghillie unfastened the boat to row me across to wade a pool from the other side. To save time I thought I would test the tension on my multiplier reel by throwing my wooden bait into the shallow water in front of me. It was immediately taken by a fresh 10-pound salmon which I had beached by the time the ghillie reached me.

Bob Grant, the ghillie at Kinnaird on the Tay, had even less reason to catch his suicidal 10-pounder.

I was looking after a lady fisher who was having a few spinning casts into the Ash Tree pool while waiting for the other guests to arrive for lunch. She hit the bank and ravelled the line into a bird's nest, so I took the rod from her and settled down to disentangle it. I pulled off the first 5 yards of line and threw it, along with the bait, into the water to get it out of the way. It was immediately seized by a fresh fish which hooked itself. There was nothing for it but to haul it in by hand, which I did. It was a welcome addition, for some of the rods who had fished expertly all morning were blank.

When I asked for a good luck story from Lady Marian Laing, wife of Lord Hector Laing, who owns a beat of the Findhorn River, her recollection was more of the 'every cloud has a silver lining' variety.

The great flood of 30 July 1956 did immense damage in Morayshire when the River Findhorn burst its banks. Our tributary, the River Divie, swept across our lawn and land, removing 6000 tons of earth and breaking the retaining wall of a large pond before finding its ways back to its course 300 yards further down. The day after the flood, however, my husband's brother and the keeper were able to net 17 salmon out of small pools left in the wreckage of our lawn. The fish had been temporarily blinded and the scales were roughened by all the boulders, stones and sand which had swept down on them.

In *Fish Tales* my friend, George Brodrick, told how, while fishing the Tweed, he had stumbled in the river and lost a gold and lapis lazuli signet ring which he greatly prized because it had never left his finger since his wife had given it to him many years previously. By what seemed a miracle the ghillie waded down the river on the following day and found it as it glinted in the sunshine.

In November 1990, George was fishing the same beat again and, while walking along a riverside wall with the same ghillie, he tripped and fell head first into the river. The ghillie quickly pulled him out, none the worse except that, once again, the signet ring had slipped off his finger and was back in the Tweed in deepish water. Once again, the ghillie's sharp eyes eventually spotted it, lodged between two rocks, and he fished it out. There will not be a third time because George swears that he will never risk fishing again without removing the precious ring.

Losing a ring, or anything else of value, in the water can be infuriating but a loss which was uniquely embarrassing befell a fishing companion of Robin Beare, the distinguished plastic surgeon who sent me his first-hand account of the incident.

The Mawddach, which runs into the sea at Barmouth, used to be a superb and prolific sea-trout river with a modest run of salmon. Its beauty, as it tumbles out of the Welsh mountains, must be unchanged but I doubt whether the same applies to the run of fish.

On a July afternoon, some 30 years ago, the river was in spate and three of us, Peter Hall, Jack the Bar (the bartender at the Golden Lion in Dolgellau) and myself, reckoned that a spinning expedition might yield a salmon. Having bought day-tickets for the Gelligemlyn water, some 3 miles from Dolgellau, it was agreed that Peter and I would fish from the right bank, with Jack on the opposite side.

After a blank half-hour I happened to cast out at the same moment as Jack and our lures, probably wooden Devons, became entangled in midstream. Jack shouted, 'Let go, Doc. I'll reel in and sort it out.' Having disentangled the two baits he shouted, 'OK. Reel in!', which I did, to the accompaniment of incoherent and, to me, inexplicable shouting from Jack. When the bait arrived at my side I was astonished to find a set of upper dentures attached to it by one hook of a treble, the shank of which had becomed jammed between the two central incisors. The denture, quite undamaged, was returned to the owner a couple of hours later, but not before he had taken a nice 5-pound grilse.

The subsequent alcoholic analysis of the episode over the bar in the Golden Lion revealed that Jack had held my monofilament line in his mouth while disentangling the spinners and had given me the OK too soon.

Apart from its beauty, the Mawddach is well known as a gold-bearing river. Drifting off to sleep that night, after a memorable day, I reflected that it would have been even better if the teeth had picked up a gold filling on the way!

An old boot is the strange catch beloved of cartoonists. Tony Richards hooked something which was rather more exciting – at first.

While standing in a position from which it was impossible for me to walk any further downstream on the bank of a good salmon stream, I hooked a monster while fishing a worm in exactly the place where a good fish should have been lying. It played hard, deep and very dour for quite a long time, and when I finally got it to the surface it turned out to be a large metal bucket with a hole in the bottom.

My husband had a similar experience when he was a boy, fishing the River Tees with maggot tackle. His hook engaged itself in one of the many holes in a large piece of corrugated iron lying on the bottom of a fast stream. It lifted off in such a lively way and appeared to be struggling so strongly, as water surged through the holes, that he was sure that he was into a salmon – so sure, in fact, that his companion took a short stroll to make sure that nobody was watching in case the fish was landed.

Inevitably, we all get our share of bad luck, usually in the form of fish which escape at the last flip, but I always console myself with the fact that you cannot lose anything before you own it and I just bid the lucky fish a fond farewell, with thanks for the fun it gave me and a special good wish: 'May you live to spawn a thousand.'

Chapter 5

The Big Ones

The classic fishing story is of the monster which 'got away' after a titanic struggle but, while it will always be the big fish that does tend to escape, some are caught under circumstances which make the success especially exciting. In recent times, the experience of Sid Rodgers of Sheffield, who kindly sent me his first-hand account of it, is in that special category.

On the morning of 16 December 1990 I arrived at Dam Flask Reservoir at 7 am and set up my tackle to fish for pike. I was using a small dead roach presented on the bottom on two Number 8 treble hooks with an 11-pound breaking strain line. It had been there for about two and a half hours without result and, as it was cold, I decided to walk down to where my two sons, Michael and Neil, were also pike fishing.

I had been there about a quarter of an hour when I heard my bite alarm sounding. I ran up to the rod, but as the alarm had stopped and my 'drop-off indicator' was still connected to the line I thought the fish had gone, if it had been there at all. Suddenly the end of the rod started to quiver and the indicator fell to the ground. I picked up the rod and waited for it to run, thinking that it was a pike, but it did not do so. By this time, Neil was by my side and I remarked, 'It's not going to run, so I'm going to hit it right away.' I wound down and struck. To my astonishment the fish leapt clean out of the water. Michael ran up shouting, 'It's a trout! Don't lose it!' Sure enough it was – a brownie so huge that I could not believe my eyes.

The trout fought harder than any pike and I slackened the clutch on my reel as I thought the line would break. It took off about 50 yards of line and after I recovered most of that it just took off again, tail-walking on the water. Four times I had it near the net and eventually, after a 10-minute fight, I lifted it out.

I did not wish to kill the fish so Neil raced up the bank to borrow a pike sack so that we could keep it alive for the bailiff to witness. Michael and I set up the Avon Dial Scales to weigh it. Neil returned not only with a sack but with three pike enthusiasts who had cameras and an identical set of scales to ours. On each set the weight was exactly the same – a staggering 17 pounds 7 ounces!

After photographs had been taken I decided not to use the pike sack, as I did not want to risk damaging such a fine specimen brown trout. Neil was given the honour of returning it and, after he had held it upright for a few seconds, we all had the pleasure and satisfaction of watching it glide safely away to live, and maybe fight, another day.

What a fish! It was a record for a wild brownie. And what a sportsman! This was catch-and-release with a vengeance. How many of us would have been able to resist taking such a fish home to be admired?

The even bigger fish caught by John Farrant, a 47-year-old game-keeper on the Minstead Manor Estate near Lyndhurst, in Hampshire, was not so fortunate. Let Mr Farrant tell the story of his red-letter day, 20 September 1992.

I was fishing in the brackish estuary of the Southampton River, which is formed by the union of the Test and the Itchen, casting for bass from a shingly beach called Calshot Point. The bait was a sand-eel and the method was like ledgering – keeping it down with a lead weight and letting it move around in the tidal water. I sensed a knock-knock on the rod tip, and from the way the fish took off about 40 yards of line it could have been a bass, but I realised that it probably was not when it sulked on the bottom for a couple of minutes and then took off again. I thought it might be a salmon, as this fish runs up both the Test and the Itchen, so I played it carefully and finally brought it to the net, which was being wielded by my companion. As it was far too big for the net, he ended up pushing the fish and the net on to the beach. I was quite sure, as soon as I saw it, that it was a sea-trout, as I had caught them up to 10 pounds. However, I greatly underestimated its weight at about 18 pounds.

As it was about 9 pm when I hooked the fish I put it in the refrigerator overnight and had it weighed next morning on the scales at my local Post Office, in Brockenhurst, and was astonished when told it weighed 28¼ pounds! I realised that this was probably an all-time British sea-trout record which, I had read, stood at about 22½ pounds. I therefore had good colour photographs taken and these were sent, along with some scales, to Dr Alwyne Wheeler, who is a scientific adviser to the British Record Fish Committee. I was delighted to receive a reply from him saying that he was in no doubt that the fish was a sea-trout – and a new record.

As permanent proof and a daily reminder of his achievement, Mr Farrant had the fish mounted – as I certainly would have done myself.

The next monster trout reported to me, a brownie, was also unfortunate because it is usually a requirement to retain such a fish on fly waters in the belief that they become cannibals. Mark Lloyd-Price reports.

I have a rod on the lower reaches of the River Test not far from Romsey, where I normally fish every Saturday. One day in July, I noticed an enormous fish in the carrier stream flowing down from a fish farm. It was almost motionless in the middle of the stream and not feeding on any surface flies. It was so big that I was unsure whether it was a trout or a salmon, and it had no interest whatever in any dry flies which I cast to it. The temptation to offer it a nymph was very strong but I resisted it as nymphs are strictly forbidden there. I also resisted an urge to wade in and try to 'tickle' it.

On the following Saturday I returned to the same spot with a guest, called Jeremy Archer, when it was so hot that the temperature at my weekend cottage on Salisbury Plain reached 95 degrees Fahrenheit in the afternoon. It was still hot when we reached the river at 8.30 pm. The big fish was still there although it had moved station, and it began to rise to a hatch of tiny midges, showing its broad back which was all of 4 inches wide – unquestionably a brown trout. Jeremy had spotted the fish first but it was rising close to our bank of the river, an impossible cast for a left-hander and a newcomer to dry-fly fishing as he was. Somewhat rudely, I suggested that he should move to the left bank over the bridge further downstream where lots of fish were rising.

For at least 15 minutes the big trout refused to take the small sedges which I was offering so, as it grew dark, I changed to a Size 14 Elk Hair sedge – a light-coloured fly often lethal in the gloaming. After several fruitless casts, there was a gentle take and a pause while I resisted the temptation to strike, followed by a strong run of 20 yards upstream. My rod and tackle were extremely light – an 8-foot split-cane fly rod given to me as a teenager and a 4-pound breaking strain tapered cast which, I discovered later, had a knot in it! So I followed the fish up the river, trying not to put too much strain on it. It moved in and out of the weeds which were mercifully not too thick and after several minutes it shot off downstream past the spot where it had been hooked towards a footbridge.

At that stage I decided to make a stand, especially as it was now quite dark and Jeremy had joined me to assist in the landing operation. Three times I brought it close enough to the bank for it to take fright from our silhouettes against the night sky. At the third attempt Jeremy extended the collapsible net a few feet behind the fish and I let the current take it tail first into the meshes. As Jeremy pulled it towards the bank the frame of the net buckled, whereupon we both grabbed it and deposited it in the field behind us. It was a hen fish 30 inches long and weighed 15³/4 pounds. It was very fat, which may explain why its fight had been steady but unspectacular.

As far as can be ascertained, after making enquiries with Mick Lunn of the Houghton Club, and with Peggy Baring, the Secretary of the Test and Itchen Fishing Association, it is a record for the Test, the next largest brownie being a 12-pounder caught on the Houghton water. I suspect that it could be the record for a fly-caught brown trout on any river in the British Isles.

Later, I discovered that the fish was well known to the employees of the local fish farm, one of whom had caught it by mistake while spinning for pike. They stock brown trout no bigger than 2¹/2 pounds so it was not a recent escapee, but had no doubt waxed fat on pellets floating down from the farm. I am having the fish stuffed by an expert who still practises the Victorian art of taxidermy.

Mr Lloyd-Price kindly sent me a colour photograph of his truly enormous fish. It took my friend Colin Farnell rather longer to appreciate the significance of his large trout.

When fishing the Leckford beat of the River Test one September in the early 1970s, I hooked and eventually landed a rainbow trout weighing 8 pounds 4 ounces after a very strong fight. I was pleased with myself because in those days, before so many big rainbows were being stocked into fishing waters, I knew it was an outstanding specimen and I had experienced quite a job dragging it over a thick bed of Ranunculus weed during a struggle which had lasted about 20 minutes.

I told a few friends about it and put the details in my own fishing diary but otherwise it was just another memorable event in the sport which has given me such pleasure over so many years. Some time later, however, while in a public reference library, I looked at a small square book about British record fish and, to my astonishment, found my name and my fish listed there as the official record for a river-caught rainbow – or perhaps any rainbow at all at that time. Of course, it has been broken many times since – in fact, I suspect that, during the height of the season these days, it is broken every week.

I suppose that Colin did not feel quite the same thrill as he would have done had he realised that it might be a record when he grassed it. My husband had a similar experience when we fishing together on the River Driva in Norway. He had never caught a 30-pound salmon, although he had been within a few ounces of it more than once in Scotland, and he was hoping to achieve that ambition on the Driva. He was delighted to catch a good fish on his first morning but estimated it at about 25 pounds. When weighed a few hours later, it was a few ounces over 31.

Shirley Deterding, the noted Norfolk sportswoman, sent me an exciting story of a record trout which, sadly, could not be counted, as Sid Rodgers' has been. It is also evidence of the importance of never missing an opportunity to go fishing, however unpromising the circumstances.

My husband, Jim Deterding, and I were staying with some friends on their ranch in Colorado and, being on the elderly side, they went off to bed for a rest after lunch. We found an old fishing rod in a cupboard and some funny-looking flies, which we later learned were called Willy Wobblers, and went off to explore the small stream which meanddered down from the mountains through their property.

We had several rises from small trout and, when the afternoon became hot and still, I decided to sit by the stream and paint a picture while Jim wandered off to see what he could find. Suddenly, while deep in concentration, I was aware of a distant and repeated shout for help. I ran down the stream and, after about half a mile, found Jim standing on the edge of a steep, muddy slope with his Mickey Mouse rod bent double. Looking into the water I could only see a thick mat of weed. 'I've got something quite big and I'm down to the last three turns of the line which has no backing,' Jim said.

I did not fancy going down near the weed with so many poisonous moccasin water snakes around, so I volunteered to hold the rod while Jim made the brave and slippery descent.

Suddenly the fish appeared midstream and it was enormous. Holding the reel tightly I brought it nearer to Jim and eventually managed to lift its head out of the water enough for him to slip his fingers into its gills and lift it clear of the weed. It was the biggest mountain trout I had ever seen and was certainly a record for that area and probably for many others.

The next problem was getting Jim and the fish up the muddy slope. I managed to tear a branch from a bush and pulled Jim up with it. The owner was highly delighted to see such a trophy from his stream but talks of having it recorded came to an abrupt end when he realised that we had no fishing licence and that it was a poached fish under Colorado law. Nevertheless it was mounted and is over the fireplace of the Lodge to this day with a plaque below giving the weight – 13 pounds – and the statement 'Caught by an Englishman'.

Not many fishermen would be disappointed to land a brown trout weighing close on 10 pounds but Roy Bush, of Richmond Surrey, was – deeply.

I was fishing a nice chub swim on the Kennet, near Ham Bridge in Newbury, and noticed a big rise handily within casting distance. I tossed my worm bait over it and it was taken immediately. The line was really solid and I knew that I was into something so big that I could feel the pulse beating in my ears. After a long fight the fish came to the net and I saw, to my intense dismay, that it was a brown trout. It weighed 9 pounds 15 ounces and had it been a chub, as I had hoped, it would easily have been a record. After being witnessed, the trout was returned. It was out of season but I cannot kill a fish anyway.

It would always be fulfilling to be able to claim a record for any fish, and most of us would be more than happy to be able to say that we had caught a 40-pound salmon, as so few have achieved that. Bruce Penney nearly did it but not quite, although he caught the fish.

Around 1979 I invited a guest, called Tubby, to fish with me for a day on the Wye, close to the town of Ross-on-Wye. He had not done much fishing before but quickly hooked a salmon and lost it. Soon afterwards he hooked a fish which we soon realised was big from the way it played, although we could not see it. My friend did not really know how to deal with such a fish and became bored, tired or both. Eventually, the salmon moved to the other side of the river and snagged the line round a groin, so we crossed in a boat to free it, which we managed to do. With the fish still on we rowed back as we were only permitted to fish from one side. Tubby then handed the rod to me to play it as he was exhausted and fed up with it.

We still had not seen the fish when it was played out but giving the rod back to Tubby to hold I managed to gaff it. The salmon was enormous. As there were no scales big enough, it could not be properly weighed until 24 hours later when it scaled 43 pounds.

Sadly neither of us could claim the fish as his capture because we had shared the playing of it.

Tubby has had enough

I imagine that, in retrospect, Bruce's friend kicked himself for not having hung on to the rod. There are plenty of instances in the annals of angling when potential records go awry even when one does all the right things, as instanced by a story supplied by Tony Ingram, formerly with the Eddington Estate fishery.

> The Eddington Estate fishery on the River Kennet at Marsh Benham, near Hungerford, awards the Craven Cup for the largest trout caught by a member of the syndicate there each season. In the 1990 season one member felt sure it was his if he could land the very large brownie he was playing. As he was trying to coax it into his net the commotion attracted the attention of an even larger pike, which siezed the trout and tore off with it.
>
> As the trout remained attached to the cast the ensuing battle was lengthy as the pike seemed disinclined to let go or was unable to, and eventually both fish came to the net. The pike weighed in at 16¹/2 pounds but sadly, about one quarter of the weight of the trout had disappeared in the fray, a reduction which put it out of contention for the Cup.
>
> It seemed sad, after such a successful battle with 20¹/2 pounds of fish, but rules are rules.

Such experiences with sea-water sharks are legion but that of Graham Rogoff is worth recording, as being typical.

> Fishing off the Seychelles, I hooked a large sailfish and when it was beaten I began to reel in the long line it had taken out in its leaping struggle, which had given me the opportunity to see how big and strong it was. The sailfish is such a game fighter that I was surprised how light it began to feel as I recovered the line. Indeed, it became easier and easier to wind it in and when it came alongside I could see why. Apart from the head, there was nothing left of the body save the skeleton!

Bruce Penney's friend Tubby may have been exhausted by his 43-pounder, but others have suffered worse fates, as Richard Warrin recalled as we sat talking in the hut on the Inchmarlo beat of the Dee, where I have enjoyed many happy hours.

> My friend Alfred Bates, a wealthy man well known in his day as the President of Essex Golf, fished on the river Usk, in Wales, as well as in Scotland. In 1977 or thereabouts I was playing in the Eccentric Knock-out and he gave me £10 to place on myself to win my next round because the bookmakers thought I was going to lose and were offering 6 to 4 against me. In fact I won and

telephoned him with the news that I had £25 for him, only to be told that he had died the day before.

It transpired that he was fishing on the Usk, got into a salmon, played it for nearly half an hour and said to the ghillie, 'I think this is the biggest fish I've ever hooked.' With that he toppled over. An ambulance was called but by the time he reached hospital he was already dead.

Eventually, a few hours later I think, the ghillie returned to the river and picked the rod up, and the fish was still on. He landed it and it weighed 34 pounds. Alfred, who had fished all his life, had never caught a 30-pounder. It was a good way for such a keen angler to go, but what a pity he had not seen it on the bank first!

In *Fish Tales* I told the story of the enormous carp, Penney, which was purchased for £2000, from the Duke of Wellington's estate, Stratfield Saye, when a pond there had to be drained after the 1987 hurricane blew down a tree which breached a dam. Penney, which weighed 37 pounds, was transferred to a coarse-fishing lake at Broadlands, where her presence brought lots of carp specialists with hopes of catching her. (I am told that such is the demand for big fish in lakes that some owners will pay £300 for a 20-pound pike!) Quite a few succeeded in catching Penney, on various baits, and put her safely back, as all coarse fishers do. In 1992 I consulted the Broadlands river keeper, Bernard Aldrich, for the latest news of Penney and he reported that, in the further hurricane of 1989, she almost certainly swam out of the flooded lake into the River Test, close by, and is probably still there, fairly immune from recapture and hopefully growing larger. Hurricanes have played quite a role in her saga.

Each time Penney was recaptured, the lucky angler could hardly wait to reweigh her and no doubt made a guess at her weight before subjecting her to the scales. It is surprising how adept one can become at judging the weight of fish with experience, as Robert Marshall, a Clackmannanshire farmer whom I met while fishing the Tay, demonstrated.

While visiting the Royal Highland Show at Edinburgh with my wife in the 1980s, we went into a tent which was selling champagne and smoked salmon sandwiches. Above and behind the counter was a large salmon in a glass case which I admired so much that the man in charge said, 'If you can guess its weight within 2 pounds I'll give you two glasses of champagne and two sandwiches.'

'Thirty-five pounds,' I answered, with a note of certainty.

'Good grief, mon! You're within half a pound', the sandwich salesman answered, filling the two glasses.

Mr Marshall did not explain that, only a few days before, while fishing the Kinnaird beat of the Tay, he had caught a 34-pounder and its size and shape were fresh in his mind.

When guessing the weight of a fresh big fish one needs to know exactly when it was caught – as witness the experience of James Klootwijk, a former President of the Flyfishers Club, when he caught his first really big salmon in Scotland.

It was Thursday in the last week of May 1987, and I was the only member of the party of five fishing the Tulchan Water on the Spey who was still blank. My allotted stretch, on B beat, was just in front of the hut where the excellent ghillie, Alan Irvine, was mowing the grass. I was just beginning to extend my fly line and on the third throw of my Silver Stoat, which was hardly intended as a proper cast, I felt a solid take. I was quickly aware that I was into a good fish, but also though my rod was bent double the ghillie continued with his mowing. After three quarters of an hour he came down, no doubt wondering why I was making such heavy weather of what he imagined was probably a nice fish but not a monster. Suddenly the fish surfaced and Alan saw its tail – the biggest he had ever seen. I also saw that the fish was well hooked in the jaw and began to give it some stick.

Over the next three quarters of an hour the salmon took us downstream about 1/2 a mile when it came into the side, beaten. The bank was a foot above the water's edge so that I could not beach it and we realised that my net was going to be too small to take it. I tried lifting it by the tail but it was too big to be gripped. Eventually Alan produced an extraordinary-looking net into which he managed to direct the fish. We got back to the hut as quickly as possible and weighed it at 35 pounds. I was so delighted that I did not fish any more but went in the search of the owner of Tulchan who joined me at the hut in a long and bibulous celebration.

By the time we had the fish weighed on more accurate scales elsewhere, before entry into the beat records, it had lost pounds so it is in as only a 33-pounder.

Pounds of a different kind were soon to come into the story because news of the fish spread up and down the river so rapidly that the hut was besieged by anglers wanting to see it. Naturally, they were happy to celebrate with me and our normally ample stocks of drink, including wine, were soon exhausted. I ordered two plaster casts of the fish, one for me and one for Tulchan Lodge, so, excluding the costs of the week's fishing I reckon that salmon cost me £650. It was worth every penny!

Big fish are not always so welcome, as for example when one catches quite a large pike when spinning for salmon, as sometimes happens on the Wye. My friend David Gardiner achieved a catch which would have made a red-letter day for millions of anglers but was just a disappointment for him.

My cousin, the late Colonel Rodney Palmer, had a marvellous arrangement whereby, every Wednesday, he had the Duke of Beaufort's Wyesham Beat of the Wye, just below Monmouth. He often used to ask me to fish there on that lovely beat, the second stretch of fast fly water up from the sea. One day, in July, I was there on my own when the water temperature was like a warm bath. After eating my lunch, following a luckless morning, I started putting my fly down the Monnow Run and suddenly I could not stop catching chub. By the time I reached the bottom I had 18 on the bank up to 4 pounds in weight – a truly miraculous draught of chub. I had reckoned that they were best out of the water, as they would be competing for food with the salmon fry and perhaps eating some of them.

Each chub was a disappointment, however, for they did not fight very well and, at the finish, the problem remained of how to dispose of them. I took them hopefully to the ghillie's house and, while he looked impressed, he wanted none of them. So I took them home and distributed them among those of my cousin's farmworkers who had cats!

No account of big fish would be complete without one that really did get away – to the chagrin of David Browse of Liss in Hampshire.

The pool is formed by the River Itchen at Gaters Mill, where the river drops 4 or 5 feet from the upper level through two hatches into the main pool below. It is only some 100 yards wide and the first 50 yards of the bank is piled and topped with concrete. Where the made-up bank finishes the river shallows, and at the end of the concrete on the right bank there is a small bushy tree overhanging the water. The rush of the main stream creates eddies on either side – to the right a small and more turbulent stream but on the left a bigger, smoother eddy, the current of which turns and sweeps back towards the hatches, hugging the bank and finally returning to the main stream where it explodes from the hatch. This was where a large salmon was lying tight against the wall.

Baiting with a red shrimp I held it close to the bank and the fish took it, slowly and very deliberately. It did only what it wanted, and I soon began to feel somewhat unnecessary to the proceedings. Eventually, it took up residence in the clear water below me and I saw that I had hooked a fish of around 30 pounds, with a tail like a spade. After three quarters of an hour it started to work its way slowly downstream and the only way I could follow it was to get round the overhanging bush. So I jumped in up to my middle and applied pressure, hoping to get the fish back into the main pool. Sadly, the salmon decided it was tired of playing with me and took off for the sea, going like a train and with no sign of fatigue. It disappeared under the wire at the bottom of the water, at which point the hook came out, leaving me very wet and very dejected.

I am told that, in theory, there is no limit to the size that a fish can reach provided it gets plenty of food in an environment conducive to growth because, unlike most other creatures, a fish does not stop growing when it becomes an adult. So those anglers who like to specialise in pursuing specimen fish have fair reason to believe that any record is capable of being broken. When this happens it is usually improved by only a few ounces, but the odds are that the record for the rainbow trout, standing at 27 pounds 2 ounces at the time of writing, will soon reach 50 pounds or even 60 – not far short of the British record for the salmon! This certainly would be a tale of the unexpected, and when I heard about it I was determined to find out if it was really possible and, if so, how it was done. So off I went to see the extraordinary man behind the ideas, Nigel Jackson, who produced that record rainbow and several before it which held the record for a short time. He has also produced a 30-pound brown trout!

The main site of his endeavours to create monster trout is on the edge of the Hampshire village of Barton Stacey, where two fairly small fishing ponds are already stocked with so many giant rainbows and browns that anglers come from as far afield as the United States, South Africa and even Australia to cast a fly at them.

Mr Jackson, who deserted his one-time love of fishing for love of fish, is such an enthusiast for growing monsters that he devotes 90 hours a week to rearing, feeding and improving them by applying all the latest developments in scientific feeding and genetics. Starting with a dry field by the River Dever, he dug the two lakes out, stocked them with brown and rainbow trout and began to issue day-tickets in June 1986. Determined to be different, he specialised in big fish from the start, believing that many anglers would pay high rates for day-tickets to try for them. He proved to be right. His lakes are usually fully let every day by early bookers throughout the six months of the normal trout season, but can be fished at other times. A day ticket costs £45 and four fish is the bag limit, but an angler who catches this quickly enough can invest another £45 for a second ticket on the same day. Many do. His take from tickets is nearing £500,000 a year, but the profit comes mainly from the fish farms which supply him. He owns those too and they produce just under 100 tons of a year – all for his own fisheries, exclusively.

Although monster fish have to be maintained on a daily diet of fish pellets, they readily take the fly, both wet and dry, which is all that is allowed, Size 10 being the limit. There is an enormous hatch of mayfly, when fast and furious sport is usually assured. Those fish which I saw, in the lakes, the stews and the photographs on the fishing hut wall, were very deep and fat and usually put up a hard fight.

Nigel Jackson's monsters are already big enough to ensure a steady trade, but he is a perfectionist driven by a desire to do even more – hence his project to produce super-monsters which he claims, astoundingly, will grow from 3 to 50 pounds in one year. By much trial and error, he is confident that he has found out exactly how to do this and he showed me round the expensive facility which he was building for the purpose. Understandably, he was reticent about giving precise details to possible competitors, but I can say that the main secret is rearing the monsters in a huge covered tank where their body temperature will be controlled at a constant 16 degrees Celsius. That, he believes, is the optimum for their growth when fed on special high-protein pellets. He achieves the heat with overhead infra-red lamps which warm the fish rather than the water and the way that this is controlled is one of his well-guarded secrets.

Mr Jackson intends to produce up to thirty 50–60-pounders this way each year to stock his lakes. He estimates that each of these monster trout could be worth up to £10,000 if he was prepared to sell them to other fisheries. So the utmost care must be taken to keep them in a sterile environment while they are being reared. This will be accomplished by ultraviolet lamps and other means. In spite of their value, however, anybody catching one will be required to keep it. Mr Jackson insists that all the fish that are caught in his lakes must be taken because he does not want to risk any infection which might result from dead fish in his ponds. He thinks that any really big trout which has fought hard, as most of them do, has suffered so much stress that its chances of survival are not good.

Not every fisherman approves of Mr Jackson's activities, as he well knows, but it is difficult to argue with him. The rearing of stock trout up to 10 pounds is common now for many commercial fisheries, rivers as well as lakes. If they can be accepted, what is wrong with 20-pounders and, by the same token, 50-pounders? Mr Jackson says that wild rainbows commonly reach this size and more, naturally, in Lake Penn in America, which he visited to see the conditions and make use of anything he could learn.

As he pointed out, those who do not wish to fish for them need not do so, and those who do can enjoy it without upsetting anybody. Those who arrive at his lakes by 9.30 in the morning can see what they are paying for as he puts in new, big fish every day. Surprisingly, at least to me, when Mr Jackson puts his fish into the lakes he *throws* them in from a height of 4 feet, I was always taught to treat them very gently. 'If they go in with a plop, they take off straight into the middle of the lake instead of hanging about, perhaps on one side, using only one gill for a while, which cannot be good for them!' he explained.

The question of the new British records which these monsters will surely set remains controversial but the British Record Fish Committee has gone far to resolve the problem by establishing two lists, one for such artificially reared fish and another for those which are wild or have been in lakes and rivers long enough to be considered as wild.

Most of us would rather fish for wild fish and fishing at Dever Springs must always be rather like fishing in a stew. But I think that we have to be realistic and recognise that in the south, at least, there are not many truly wild fish and most of those we catch began life in stews. The rainbows, in particular, have not usually been in the river for long. So I may not be able to resist having a go for a 50-pounder once they are available. After all, the 10½ pound rainbow which I caught in the Kennet on a small nymph, and of which I was so proud because it was a new record for the beat, had been in the river for only a few weeks.

Chapter 6

Long Odds

I guess that the odds against finding a fresh fish in the middle of a large grass field, as my husband did, are pretty high but so many of the things that happen out fishing are against all odds. Take the true story supplied by Norman Sinclair, the ghillie of the Little Blackhall beat at Banchory, which has given my husband and me many hours of pleasure.

> A few years ago, in the spring, a salmon was lost to a bait fisher on the opposite beat, Inchmarlo, and the line had broken by the small ball-bearing swivel. So the fish had escaped with the bait in its mouth and a few feet of nylon with a swivel attached to its end trailing behind it in the water. A day or two later, my predecessor, Rod Grant, was fishing a bait on the Little Blackhall side and one of the hooks on his treble bait penetrated the eye of the swivel of the lost fish. He landed the fish which weighed about 10 pounds.
>
> The aperture of the swivel's eye measures 2 millimetres. Further, the swivel was almost certainly waving about in the current behind the fish. So the odds against such a meeting of hook and eye must be so high as to be incalculable.

While the chances against such an event happening in a river are high, they must be even more remote in a huge lake such as Kariba in Zimbabwe, but something like it happened to Senator P.K. van der Byl (always known to his many friends as 'P.K.').

> On the first day of a holiday in Zimbabwe, then Southern Rhodesia, I took my mother-in-law, Elizabeth of Liechtenstein, tiger fishing in the estuary of the Sengwa River where it enters the Kariba Lake. It is a featureless stretch of water, apart from the fact that it is enormous. In the course of the morning, while fishing from a boat with a spoon-bait, a large tiger fish broke me as it flung itself out of the water although I was using a stranded-steel trace.
>
> On the second day we went hunting but fished again from a boat on the third. Among the tiger fish I hooked and landed was one with my broken trace and spoon still hanging from its mouth. There was no doubt about it – I could recognise the binding.

The tiger fish is so aggressive – hence its name – that catching the same fish twice was, perhaps, not remarkable in itself, but to do so in that immense tract of water containing thousands of tiger fish certainly was.

My American friend Art Whitcombe went one better in the vastness of the ocean, as he told me while we were salmon fishing together at Kinnaird in September 1990.

A friend and I were catching blue fish off Long Island and I heard on the local radio that someone else had hooked and lost a small swordfish. I happened to look back and saw that our lines were in a mess, so we started to reel in to put things right. Suddenly, from the bill sticking out of the water, I realised that we were playing a swordfish. Eventually we brought it to the side and sure enough it was the fish which had been hooked and lost miles away. We had entangled the line it had broken. The chances against this happening in the open ocean must have been astronomical.

Many anglers have had the uncommon experience of landing a trout and hooking it again on the same day, but Stanley Marber probably set a record for long odds when fishing the little River Alre near Alresford in Hampshire.

Nymphing with a small artificial shrimp, I cast at a good brown trout lying between some weeds, rose it and I tried to hold it near the surface. The fish shook the hook loose and went straight back to its lie. With little hope of success, I immediately put the same shrimp over the trout, which rose and took it more forcibly. Again, to keep it out of the weeds, I put maximum pressure on it and the fish seemed solidly hooked. Once again, however, it shook the fly free.

I waited behind a tree for a few minutes while I took stock of this intriguing situation and decided that it might just be worth trying again, but with a slightly different shrimp. At the first cast the fish banged at the fly and really took it so that after a good fight I was able to net it – a $2^3/4$ pounder, a fine fish for this little river.

While fishing the Tay at Kinnaird, I met Eric Thorburn, a Scottish photographer and keen angler, who related a story of the same genre.

Every year a small group of us go to the island of Jura to fish some lochs there which contain really wild brown trout. In one of them there is a shingle island about 10 feet in diameter which can just be reached in waders. One of our party, Donald Forrester, was fishing wet fly from it one morning when he hooked a very lively fish which fought hard, taking him round the island several times and finally breaking the very fine cast and escaping with one of the three wet flies.

On the afternoon of the same day another member, Joe Stirling, the Editor of the *Scottish Field*, hooked a lively fish and landed it. For that loch it was a big one – 1½ pounds – and there, in the corner of its mouth, was the fly which Donald had lost a few hours earlier. Joe had the pleasure in making a formal presentation of it that evening. I have heard of stock trout being hooked twice, but for such a wild fish it must have been unusual.

A rather extraordinary variation on this theme was related to me by David Gardiner.

I had my cousin, Malcolm Fraser, fishing with me on my beat of the Lambourn, just below Boxford. During the morning I was fishing near the top of the beat using a Kite's Imperial, which I always found to be the most successful fly on that river. Seeing a wild trout rising, I cast over it and hooked it but it promptly weeded me. Lambourn fish do not grow very big but they are very sporting, and where there is a good growth of Ranunculus they will weed you quicker than you can blink. I tried everything I knew to dislodge the fish but finally the cast came back minus the fly. So we retired for lunch.

When we returned to the river, Malcolm fished where I had lost my trout, also using a Kite's Imperial. He too got into a fish which weeded him and, as I was not far below, he called for help. I waded in and gently ran my finger and thumb down his cast. Sadly, as I reached the fly it came free but there was a consolation – for me, at least. Attached to his Kite's Imperial, hook to hook, was another Kite's Imperial – undoubtedly the one I had lost a few hours before.

Many coarse fish which are returned to the water after being caught are captured again after an interval of a few days or longer. So the rather ridiculous situation has arisen in which a record fish is returned then recaptured a few weeks later, by which time it may have grown by a few more ounces, so creating a new record.

This happened with a barbel which weighed 14 pounds 13 ounces when caught in 1992 and 15 pounds 1 ounce when caught again a couple of months later, as the lucky angler records in detail elsewhere in this book. As it was returned unharmed once more there could, of course, be no end to the saga.

Normally a decent interval elapses before the same fish takes again but by no means always.

Martin Porter of Staines was pike fishing in a gravel pit with two rods out, each baited with a dead sprat. A big pike took one of them and while he was playing it he wound in the other line as much as he could. After a stiff fight he landed the pike, carefully removed the hook, weighed it – a hen fish of 25 pounds – photographed it and held it in the water for a few minutes while it recovered. He then gently pushed it out into the deeper water when it spied the other sprat lying on the bottom by the side. It made a dive for it, grabbed it, hooked itself and had to be played again, putting up a decent fight once more.

That fish seemed to be either suicidal or at least, masochistic but I recently heard of a trout which was caught three times in one day. Peter Garvan, who lives near Swindon, was fishing for roach and dace with bread in a carrier of the River Kennet not far from the back of our house when he caught a rainbow of about $2^1/2$ pounds. The fish was easily recognisable because its dorsal fin was so deformed that it was little more than a stump. It was returned unharmed and, as Mr Garvan continued to fish in the same place, it was recaptured twice. Two days later, he and a friend returned to fish again. Each of them caught the trout yet again. It had taken bread five times in three days, no doubt because it was so hungry that the need for food overcame its natural caution. The month was January, a bad time for natural food in a trout stream.

I was not surprised that the fish liked bread. By nature any trout is a carnivore but it is also an opportunistic feeder. Where I fish, the hut where we have lunch or supper is set athwart the Kennet with a picture window on each side. It is customary to throw any remaining bread into the stream to watch the monsters rise from the deep water to rive at it. If only they would rise to a fly like that! I was surprised, however, to learn from Mr Garvan that in some of the reservoirs near London the most attractive bait for a trout is sweetcorn!

Sometimes when unlikely events occur, it can pay to take them in one's stride as though they were common enough, as Richard Evanson, the owner of the famous Turtle Island resort in Fiji described to me.

I was running a game-fishing boat from Fiji, and a couple who wished to hire it asked me if I could guarantee that the lady would catch a sailfish – something she had always wanted to do – and that her partner would catch a shark on a trolling bait. I knew that the odds against this were enormous on both counts. No sailfish had been caught in the area for a year and, while sharks commonly snap at fish being played on trolling baits, they are hardly ever landed because they just go off with half the fish. However, being unwilling to turn away custom, I said with unwarranted confidence that, while catches could never be guaranteed, anything was possible in the Fiji game-fishing grounds.

Within an hour of fishing the lady hooked and landed a sailfish of about 80 pounds. Not long afterwards her husband hooked a small tuna of about 20 pounds which was grabbed by a shark. By some enormous fluke the shark not only took the whole fish but the hook as well, and was brought to the gaff. It weighed in at 120 pounds.

I had two well-satisfied customers and shrugged off their achievements as all in a day's fishing off Fiji.

A rather similar and equally satisfying episode was experienced by Sebastian Santa Cruz, son of the distinguished diplomat who was Chilean Ambassador in London for many years, and who is a purist flyfisher.

I fish, regularly, in a lake in Chile which is well stocked with rainbow and brown trout, which breed naturally in the feeder streams, as these are well supplied with the cold water which the rainbow eggs need. One day, happening to be short of available fly-fishing friends, I invited a couple of ironmongers – my name for those who throw metal baits about – to join me on my boat. They caught a few fish but I was determined, if I could, to convert them to the true way of life. So I insisted that one of them should use my equipment, telling him that a fish caught on a dry fly – something he had never even tried before – would not only give him more fun but greater satisfaction. I showed him what to do and on his very first cast, a short one which he accomplished reasonably well, he rose, hooked and landed an 8-pound rainbow.

Whoever is the god of fly fishers, he was on my side that day and I had an immediate convert.

Mr R. Edmonds has supplied me with details of an odds-against event which must, surely, be unique.

When I came to view a stretch of the River Chess near Chorleywood, with a view to buying it, the agent and the river keeper walked it with me, the latter carrying his rod in case he saw a chance to show me that it held good brown trout. At one big bend he thought he saw a fair trout rise and put his fly over it. The fish took it and, as the keeper tightened, unduly firmly I thought, the fish suddenly emerged from the water. To my amazement it was a goldfish of the size one might win in a bowl at a fairground and, with the keeper's mouth wide open in astonishment, it landed slap between his teeth.

The agent hastily explained that there was a tropical fish farm

An exotic mouthful

lower down the river from which the goldfish must have escaped, although I suppose that someone might have put the fish there having decided that it was unwanted. Anyway, I bought the stretch and have enjoyed it for more than 30 years. We have never hooked another goldfish, however.

Chapter 7

Total Immersion and Other Embarrassments

When *Fish Tales* was ready for publication, my publisher showed me a blurb which he was sending out to booksellers. To my surprise and annoyance I read that while I had been salmon fishing on a beat of the Tay I had lost my footing and fallen into the deep water. No such thing had ever happened and I objected because all the stories in the book – including the blurb – had to be true in my opinion. The publisher argued that if it was not true it would be one day because every angler falls in at some time. How right he proved to be!

The very next season I was fishing the Tay on the water now belonging to Kinnaird House, which has been turned into a luxurious hotel by my friend, the owner, Mrs Connie Ward. As my husband is such an experienced fisherman we were without a ghillie as we both fished down the lovely Guay pool. In any event, a ghillie would not have been of much use in my predicament because I have never met one who can swim.

My husband, who was following me down the pool about 80 yards upstream, kept an eye on me as I waded deep along the gravelly bottom, casting out towards the far bank, where I had seen a salmon show. We were both wading more cautiously than usual, because, just a few weeks previously, a member of our trout-fishing syndicate who was only in his mid-sixties, fit and full of river experience, had drowned on the Spey. Suddenly my left foot slid into a deep hole and I felt my chest waders filling with water. I managed to stand on one leg, but then fell forward over a large boulder which I did not know was there. I was out of my depth and dragged down by my waterlogged waders.

There is a widespread belief that past events flash through the mind of a drowning person, but mine was filled with the story of our poor friend who had gone under, never to return, in fairly calm water and in circumstances which, from the bank, initially looked laughable. I also recalled an even more horrific tale, told to me by Mrs Rose Gundry, about a man and his wife who had been fishing different pools of the Wye, with the lady wading in the upper pool. The man noticed what he believed to be a large waterlogged paper parcel floating close by him and gaffed it out to find that it was his wife, upside down and full of water! Fortunately, I also remembered the drill – that one should get on one's back with one's arms outstretched and hopefully float and paddle oneself towards the shore with one's hands. I was getting nowhere fast, but fortunately my husband had quickly spotted my predicament and was racing down the shingle as fast as his waders would let him. Our chocolate Labrador, Dido, who was pegged down on the bank, was also making quite a commotion and was clearly trying to get to me.

I think that, as I heard him shouting encouragement, I was more afraid that he would get a heart attack than I was of drowning, but I was greatly relieved when I felt his arms round me. Somehow, working together, he heaved me out to safety on the bank. It is odd how quickly fear vanishes once one is safe, and both our thoughts were for my rod and reel which had disappeared into the river when I had decided to try to float. His bait rod was on the car, nearby, and while I shivered on the bank he fished for it and managed to hook it at the third cast.

When I got back to Connie's house the ghillie remarked, laconically, 'Ah you went into Dick's Hole', named after the first person who had stumbled into it. He had not warned me about it because he never expected I would be wading so deep. Clearly he did not know my determination when I have seen a fish show!

The publisher's prediction had certainly been fulfilled with a vengeance but there is always something to be learned out fishing and that lesson was not to wade without a stick, however level the bottom may seem. My friend Caroline Pratt of Bothamstead, near Newbury, made the same mistake, although in such hilarious circumstances that it almost seemed worthwhile.

I would like to be able to say that I was playing the fish of a lifetime all through the ensuing episode but that was not the case. Instead, I was fishing a beat of the Spey which not only looked and felt entirely devoid of salmon but in the blazing drought of 1991 undoubtedly was. My efforts could hardly be described as fishing, for all I was doing was going through the motions in the line of duty – shuffling idly along after every second lackadaisical cast in water not much above my knees and wondering how soon I could decently head towards the bank and a big gin and tonic.

In fact, the only thing that had kept me going that long was a large gathering of wedding guests on the opposite bank, where the churchyard comes right down to the water. A lot of them were watching me watching them, perhaps with a certain degree of envy, for I had to be a lot cooler than they were in their finery, even if the chances of a fish were non-existent.

The bride and bridegroom were standing to one side, involved in a lengthy and rather self-conscious session with the official photographer. Eventually, the details were agreed and pictures of the bride in white and the groom in his kilt and all that goes with it, looking rather resplendent in the bright sunshine, were quickly taken for the family record. The bride had her back to the river when it came to her turn to be pictured on her own and there must have been some difficulty about getting her to smile because the groom, who had placed himself behind the photographer, proceeded to entertain her with his own version of a Highland fling, with many high kicks with his kilt uplifted. Sadly, from my position in the river with the photographer impeding my view I still do not know the answer to the perennial question, although judging by the total collapse of the bride, she, at least, was left in no doubt. The photographer, under his black hood, remained oblivious to the pantomime and my own inattentiveness caught up with me as I tripped over a submerged stone and fell face down into the river after desperate attempts to regain my balance, which must have amused the bridegroom as much as his antics had cheered me. Shallow it may have been but the Spey current is fierce and I was quite a few yards downstream before I managed to get up again, still clutching my rod, but watching all my belongings in the pouch in front of my waders disappear into deep water.

It is never safe to take liberties with a salmon river, which demands attention at all times, so my husband and I have both invested in gas-inflatable waistcoats and will never enter the water, or even fish off the bank of a salmon river, again without them. So far, we have not needed to activate them. Should that eventuality occur I hope that we make a better job of it than Ted Allaman, an American businessman and salmon-fishing friend.

While fishing in Iceland, I had been given a sealed tube which could be inflated by a gas cartridge to help keep me afloat if I fell into the river. The cartridge was inside my felt-soled waders, which I had also been advised to tie up with a belt round my body. All was going well until my hat blew off and I tried to pick it up. I pitched forwards into the water and – you guessed it – the cartridge went off! It blew my waders up like a balloon and the current carried me off. For no sensible reason, I found my rather dangerous predicament highly amusing and I was laughing so much that I almost went over a waterfall. Fortunately I came to my senses, realised my true situation and managed to paddle myself out.

Happily, most total immersions end in laughter, as witness the story told me by Philip Farley, another New York businessman, whom I met fishing in Scotland. He was invited to fish for salmon with Lord Brabourne, who showed him various pools and their holding places and hazards. He pointed out one particular place in a pool which Philip was going to fish first and advised that, because there was a large hole there, it was essential to prod ahead with one's wading stick. Philip obeyed his instructions and negotiated the hazard successfully. On looking upstream he saw that his lordship was following him down the pool. The next time he glanced in that direction it was to see Lord Brabourne staggering out of the water wet through after falling into the very hole.

My husband and I have both noticed that ghillies have little sympathy for anglers who take no notice of their warnings about the dangers on their beats, but we have not come across one quite so phlegmatic as a certain Campbell encountered by Dr Michael Simpkiss, a retired paediatrician who lives in Poole, Dorset, and is probably the keenest salmon angler I have met.

I was fishing with a ghillie called Campbell on the Spey, in a pool called the Battery. As I entered the water he warned me, 'This is a dangerous place.' Asked if there had been any unfortunate accidents, he said 'I will tell you and the other guests about that at the end of the day.' We fished the pool out together without anything untoward happening. As my host and I were putting the rods in the rod-box at the end of the day, Campbell appeared and we asked him to tell us about the dangers of the Battery pool.

He said, 'I mind the time I was fishing one spring morning with a gentleman who said he had a lot of experience and didn't want any help at all. I pointed out that this was a dangerous pool because, some yards out, there is a sudden drop from a ledge and a dangerous undercurrent. It was therefore wise that I should accompany him. He said nothing and we set out to fish. A few paces from the ledge I steadied his arm and said 'Do not go any further, sir. In three paces you'll be up to your neck.' He replied with a grunt, indicating that he needed no help from me and stepped forward boldly after fishing out the cast. He began to take another step forward. Again I steadied his arm and stopped him, saying, 'You are now on the edge of the ledge, sir. You must haul back and must return to the shore.'

'However he was stubborn and shook off my arm. In doing so he stepped forward again.' At that point Campbell paused. We said, 'What did you do Campbell?'

He replied: 'Well, sir, I turned ma back and kindled ma pipe for I canna bear to watch a man droonin.'

59

'*I canna bear to watch a man droonin*'

Fortunately it transpired that although the angler was washed away down the pool, he emerged at the bottom, cold and badly shaken. He has not fished there since.

Dr Simpkiss achieved almost total immersion himself but by design, though the outcome could have been rather embarrassing, especially for such a professional figure.

One hot, sunny day I was fishing the Rookery beat at Broadlands. In those days the other side was a private beat for the house and the salmon tenants, of whom I was one, fished from the right bank. There was a pool called the Ash Tree and above the tree which gave the pool its name was a small platform, while on the other side of the stream was a deep, short gut, which was a good lie. There was a lot of weed in the river and in order to cover the lie, it was necessary to cast a line of about 30 yards over it. I did this and hooked a fish. Usually a fish hooked there would run down the clear water on the other side, when it was then necessary to pass the rod round the ash tree and come to terms with the fish in a lower pool called the Trees pool.

On this occasion, however, the fish moved into the outer rim of a long patch of cut and dead weed extending into the river for about 5 yards. I managed to get the rod round the tree but could not move the salmon. Indeed, any attempt to do so would only have pulled it further into the tangled weed.

I looked round and, as there was nobody in sight, I decided to go in after the fish as the only alternative to losing it. I stripped off all my clothes, and walked into the river, which was quite deep and very cold, and in due course hand-lined the fish gently so that it went down into the Trees pool where I would be able to deal with it. All I had to do was to get on to the bank, slip some clothes on and play the fish. Unfortunately, at that moment I heard voices and while nobody was in sight I thought it prudent to stay put in the water. Looking very carefully upstream, I spotted Lord Mountbatten with some of his family strolling slowly down the bank towards me.

I managed to move towards a tree, and as I was then so deep in the water that only my head was showing I considered that I was likely to be invisible as long as I kept still. The family walked down the other side of the river slowly as they chatted, and when they were opposite me I began to shiver so much that the entire weed bed undulated like an Atlantic swell. I had to wait a long time until I had judged that they had reached Beat 1 and were completely out of sight before I dared move. Furthermore, I had to be certain that they were not followed by anyone else. All was well. I nipped out of the river very quickly and the fish, which weighed 14 pounds, was safely netted while I was still naked.

I wonder what would have happened had Lord Mountbatten seen that head sticking out of the water. It is a pity he did not – it would have made me an even better story!

At least Dr Simpkiss was able to keep his embarrassment private, unlike Ray Hammond, a dedicated all-round fishermen whom I met fishing the canal near our house.

I was on the Wiltshire Avon, near Amesbury, for the evening trout rise and was annoyed to see that all the cattle from the other side were in the water, muddying the stream and generally ruining the prospects. As I had cycled a long way and the farmer was a friend, I waded across and walked to his home. He and his daughter very kindly came down to the river and drove them out, saying that I had done him a good turn because the river was starting to rise, which was rather unusual for such a chalk stream.

Confident that I could still get across to the other bank, I waded in but I was soon up to my neck and had to swim the last few yards. There was nothing for it but to pack up and cycle home to dry off. It was a rotten evening's sport, but there was worse to come. For some reason, the local policeman became very suspicious of this dripping wet stranger riding a bike and wanted to know all the details of what I had been up to. By the time I was able to convince him that my story was true I was chattering with cold.

Another angler who had a bovine encounter ending in total immersion would, no doubt, have kept quiet about it, in the circumstances, but it was witnessed by one of my informants, Roy Bush of Richmond, Surrey. This gentleman was so tall and thin that when he huddled on the bank watching his float he reminded his companions of a vulture. Mr Bush and others went to his assistance when he cried out for help, to find him stretched out into the water grasping the two horns of a cow which was in midstream. It seemed that the cow had been intent on crossing the river and emerging where the gentleman was fishing. To prevent that, he had literally taken the cow by the horns. Regrettably the cow had gone a few steps into reverse and the angler was arched out over the water. As Mr Bush approached in the hope of resolving his predicament, the cow took a further step backwards and gravity intervened. The gentleman ended up face down in the river – a real Laurel and Hardy situation.

I have never seen a ghillie or river keeper fall in, but they are not immune, as Bob Bailey, who runs the Barton Court fishery behind our house related.

I had just taken over the fishery and spent the first day mowing the verges. All was going well until the mower ran away with me. I suppose that I should have let go but, being determined to try to stop it, I hung on and it took me into the river with it, up to my waist in the water.

With the help of some fishermen, I retrieved the mower, as well as myself, and knew that by taking it apart all that I would lose would be time. What I had forgotten, however was that my £200 portable telephone was in my pocket and was a write-off. An expensive morning's work!

Dave Phipps of Epsom, in Surrey, owed his soaking to a fish.

I was fishing at night for barbel on the Kennet at Aldermaston, in Berkshire. The bailiff came round at midnight, accompanied by a Rottweiler dog, and although I belonged to the Association owning the fishing rights he demanded to see my membership card. It was a nuisance because I had to climb up a bank, leaving my rod on its rest. I had not had a bite but, sure enough, while I was dealing with the bailiff a big barbel took my bait and jerked my rod off its stand into the water. There was just enough moonlight for me to see at least £200 of tackle going down the river. There was just one thing for it – to run down the bank, stripping off as I went because I knew that I would have to swim in to get it. I managed to do so, many yards downstream after crossing a fence, a stile and a cattle-drink but sadly the fish had gone.

It may sometimes be an innocent observer who gets the wetting as Dr R.B. Broughton recalled for me.

It was a cloudless winter's day without a breath of wind when the fishing club working party gathered on the bank of a little limestone river in Lancashire, then noted for its salmon, sea-trout and brown trout. One tree was eyed by all. It stood on the opposite bank, not really our property, but one of its thick twin trunks arched right over the river, reaching above our side, and had ensnared more than its share of flies.

One brave and desperate spirit waded across, clambered up and began his heinous work with the saw. He was only halfway through when a local was espied, walking with his dog on our bank. We all stopped work and gathered in a nonchalant stance on our side of the river, admiring the view. The branch creaked under its weight.

The local stopped and gave us good-day. A mild, and hopefully short, conversation was struck up. The branch creaked a little

more. The amiable dog had found new friends and was loath
to leave them. Again the ominous creaking, but there was no
hurrying the man and his dog standing on the edge of the stream.
Finally, with an ear-splitting crash, the trunk split and fell, creating
a tidal wave which engulfed the lower parts of both the local and
his dog.

The dog yelped back to the village as we wiped his owner
down. There was silence until a voice from the back murmured,
'By heck, you get some mighty strong winds in these parts.'

The liquid which the unfortunate angler encounters may not always
be water as John Drewett, a noted collector of ancient fishing tackle
reported.

It was the fishing club's Christmas outing and we were pacing up
and down the pavement in the bitter cold, awaiting a coach which
should have picked us up at 6 am. Eventually we heard the throaty
chug accompanied by a crashing of gears and our hopes that we
might have been allotted a 'good one' were shattered as the vintage
coach trundled into view; no coach operator would willingly send
one of his better vehicles to transport 35 men wearing studded
waders or wellies to a muddy riverbank and back home again.

The coach rattled on through the countryside, which was white
with frost, towards our venue on the Thames. 'Pity you chaps are
all going to suffer from cold feet today,' one of the anglers, called
Arthur, smirked as he lifted his legs into view. He was wearing a
splendid pair of government surplus flying boots which his wife
had given him as an early Christmas present.

'Just wait until you get them muddy,' his friend Johnny
observed.

'No problem today,' Arthur replied. 'The frost's too hard.'

We gathered our gear and prepared for the long trudge
towards a grassy mound which could either be surmounted or
circumnavigated. 'There's an easier way through the farmyard,'
Arthur declared, clomping off in the lightening dawn. Suddenly
he faltered and his indecisiveness caused those following him
to stop. 'Oh no! Oh bugger!' he wailed as he dropped with a
loud crack 2 feet into the ground and an evil smell wafted down
from his direction. He had strayed on to the frozen top of the
farm's settling pond and his precious fur-lined boots filled with
foul slurry.

Poor Arthur! Although he gradually became accustomed to the
smell the rest of us complained bitterly on the way home.

When Tom Quinn, the angling writer and editor, travelled by train to fish the Thames, it was not so much the smell as the sight of the objects for which he was responsible that made him unpopular.

> While on my way to fish for roach and chub at Goring, I was staring contentedly out of the window when I noticed that further down the carriage, in which almost every seat was taken, passengers were leaping about, screaming and shouting. I took no notice at first but as the cries of outrage and disgust grew louder I eventually noticed that my big tub of extra large maggots had tipped over and thousands of them had rolled and crawled along the carriage. The passengers were jumping around to avoid them but they were absolutely everywhere. What could I do? Only one thing. I hid my tackle bag and what remained of my maggot supply under the seat and pretended to be asleep.

A different kind of embarrassment befell Keith Speer of St Albans.

> I was trout fishing from a boat in Lough Mask in Ireland, which I do regularly each year because the big trout there are wild. I hooked and lost a good fish and gave vent to my annoyance by a loud; '– it!' To my astonishment I suddenly realised that the two men in the boat not far away, who had undoubtedly heard my remark, were priests. Although fishing as hard as I was, they were wearing their dog collars. I felt too embarrassed to apologise. Fortunately, when one of them rose a fish and failed to hook it, he let rip with exactly the same expletive. I felt absolved.

With respect to expletives on the water, my husband is an expert and, if the moment is right, nobody is spared. For many years he has been a fishing companion of Lord Sieff, but the latter came in for some bitter words while he was spinning a bait down the Swimming Pool stream on the Kinnaird beat of the Tay, desperately trying to get a fish on a blank day. He felt a wonderful tug and the feeling of something heavy and alive but, within a few seconds, realised that all was not well. Eventually he reeled in a plastic shopping bag half filled with water. 'Bloody Marks and Spencer!' he cried as he disengaged the hooks.

Sir Jan Lewando, the great authority on textiles and keen salmon fisher, tells an embarrassing story of his early days in Southend where he managed one of Marks and Spencer's stores.

> I became the Secretary of a little sea-fishing club and it was my duty to arrange the boat to take us out towards the Nore lightship which was our best fishing ground, providing dabs, flounders, cod and other delicacies. I was also responsible for certain other jobs, such as ensuring that everything was available for making the tea, including a supply of fresh water. We had two kettles, which

happened to be identical, one for boiling the water for the tea, the other for dealing with the minor call of nature. A kettle is ideal for the latter purpose since it can be used to give some degree of privacy and has a spout so that its contents can be disposed of in the sea. Regrettably, on one occasion, I mixed up the kettles and was asked to resign.

The embarrassment related by my friend and neighbour, the fish farmer Michael Stevenson, did not happen on the water, although that was the intended location.

An old man who had fished with us on the Kennet stated in his will that he wished his ashes to be spread on the river, and his wife asked me to undertake the task. Returning from the crematorium, I called in at a garage in Hungerford to get fuel and the pump attendant, whom I knew, asked me what I had been doing that day. When I explained, he asked to be shown the urn and the ashes, as he had never seen any before. I lifted the lid and, at that moment, a great gust of wind blew half the ashes across the forecourt, which was hardly what the deceased had desired. The balance of the ashes did go into the Kennet, but I often wondered which part of him went on to the forecourt.

A similar experience befell one of the ghillies on the Delfur beat of the Spey owned by Sir Denis Mountain, who told me the story.

An angler who had fished the beat for many years requested in his will that he be cremated and his ashes scattered in his favourite pool, which was called Beaufort. It was a windy day when the ceremony was performed and as the lid of the urn was lifted the ash blew into the faces of those close to it. 'Och! He always was an awkward bugger!' the head ghillie was heard to exclaim.

As a salmon fisher who has favourite pools, I can understand such a last request, but the instructions left by the owner of a shoot went a little too far for my taste. He ordered that his ashes should be loaded into cartridges to be supplied to his shooting companions who would discharge them in a *feu de joie*.

Chapter 8

Confessions

I fear there have been many occasions – and no doubt there will be more – when salmon have been deliberately gaffed or snagged out by frustrated fishermen anxious not to return to base empty-handed. Most culprits keep their secret to themselves for ever but John Noble, the owner of Ardkinglas Estate at Cairndow in Argyllshire, has sent me his delightful confession.

The day dawned bright with hope and anticipation. My cousin Iain and I were staying at Inverchorachan, an old disused shepherd's cottage far up Glen Fyne. The Smiths, our fishing tenants on the Fyne, had asked us to join them on the top half of the river for the day. It had rained hard in the night and the river was falling. Everything felt right; confidence was high.

It was to be a fly-only day, I decided. I was nearly 15 and worming seemed too puerile to contemplate. An old flybook, leather bound, heavily strapped, carried my modest stock of flies, all recently purchased, and I felt sure that Margaret Smith, an expert fisherwoman, would approve of my choice.

I had been allocated the Cottage pool and the Midge. The Cottage was my best bet and I cycled the 1¹/₂ miles there in record time. When my first cast with a Blue Charm wrapped itself round a stanchion of the bridge, I knew that my 8-foot greenheart, wielded with limited skills, would be fully stretched to cover the river, narrow as it was. And so it proved. Somewhat deflated, I moved up to the Midge, where things were better. The usual cloud of insects which give the pool its name were cowed by the wind, and near the tail I hooked a fish. All went well until, with the fish coming to the gaff for the second time, the fly came out. Snivelling with disappointment, I made my way upstream to the Laraig pool where Iain and Margaret Smith were fishing. Iain had caught a 4-pound grilse and was trying the pool down again. 'What a pretty line Iain throws,' said Margaret. I agreed in a toneless voice.

Suddenly he was into another fish which turned out to be a fresh 8-pound salmon with sea-lice. No one could be less sincere than an empty-handed fisherman congratulating a friend flushed with success. 'Great!' I grunted as we ate our lunch-time piece.

My decision had already been made – back to the worm tin in the afternoon and to hell with the niceties. Yet all in vain. By the time the evening was on me no fish had done more than chew at my worm. Indeed, salmon parr had feasted freely on the bait, but there was no serious interest from adult fish. My last chance was the Pot, a resting place in the falls where fish can lie in numbers in a confined space. A choice, well-dangled worm often hooked a fish there with not too many questions asked. As I moved on to the rocky ledge close to the Pot I saw in the Split, just above it, an enormous tail break the water as a fish turned round in the nearest shallow end. The Split is little more than another ledge forming part of a natural salmon ladder up the falls. Never did Captain Ahab stare at Moby Dick with more excitement than I at that great wide tail as it disappeared again into deeper water.

A nefarious plan to save the day sprang to my mind. Putting down my rod, I whipped out my gaff and opened it fully. I sidled down to the Split over slippery rock, half-blinded by the spray, and peered forward as I was certain that the big salmon would turn round again. It did, and this time I could see half its massive back. Reaching far out with the gaff, I struck into the water just where I guessed its shoulder would be. It was no contest. If I had hooked my gaff round the tow bar of our tractor when it was doing 20 miles an hour it could not have been ripped from my grasp more effortlessly. There was a flash of broad silver flank and the monster had hurtled back into the Pot in the twinkling of an eye, gaff and all.

The next day, Charles Smith, worming in the pool below the falls, had a bite and played what he thought was a salmon for nearly a minute in the fast, deep water at the top of the pool. To his astonishment he discovered that he had, in fact, hooked my gaff. As this was his only excitement of the morning he did not hide his irritation at my managing to 'drop' the gaff in the pool. Colin, our head deer stalker then gave me back the incriminating instrument still open, with an expression on his face which clearly said, 'I ken fine what you were up to.'

Colin was a kind man and I knew that he would not 'clype' on me to my father but I felt I had let him down badly. I had stooped to the basest of poaching methods – what shame and humiliation I felt. He must have noticed it because a day or two later he chose to tell me the true story of the capture of the Fyne's record fish, the legendary 30-pounder. Of course I knew this fish well. I had often admired, with awe, its portrait hanging in the porch room.

A nefarious plan

It was a fish of enormous length. In front of its nose a large Jock Scott had been painted and the fish, to my youthful imagination anyway, seemed to have a faintly mysterious smile playing round its gills like some piscine Mona Lisa nursing a secret.

In the early 1920s, so the story ran, my grandfather was staying with his family at Glen Fyne Lodge. It had been a cloudless 10 days and the nearest anyone had got to fishing was to make daily inspection of a monster fish lying halfway across Strutt's pool in the little bit of deep water that the trickle of river provided. Long were the late-night debates about its size. Some thought about 20 pounds; others, after three or four brandies, talked it up to 40. Bets were taken.

Although the sun continued to blaze, my grandfather surprised everyone one morning by going off fishing with old Archie MacCallum, Colin's father. Within an hour they returned with Archie struggling under the weight of a formidable salmon. Hung on the scales in the larder it turned them at 30 pounds exactly. The largest fish ever landed on the Fyne had just been taken.

Colin's eyes twinkled as he told me, 'It was caught on a white fly.' I looked perplexed so he explained the method. 'You tie on a large treble hook and attach a small strip of white cloth above it. Then you wrap some lead wire close to the hook. You approach the bank gingerly until you see the salmon clearly and then cast out well beyond the fish without splashing. The white cloth lets you see where the treble is lying and you steadily work it in as close as possible to the fish's head. Then you strike sideways hoping to foul-hook the salmon somewhere around the gills.'

I was struck dumb. So the revered grandfather, baronet of the realm, Balliol scholar, collector of old silver, public benefactor and, above all, catcher of the Fyne's record fish had foul-hooked it – the Jock Scott in the picture notwithstanding.

A wave of relief washed over me, as wise Colin knew it would. Though Izaak Walton enjoins all true anglers to be 'lovers of virtue', it seemed that we are all human. Fishermen both old and young could stray from the straight and narrow. I felt a sense of companionship with this grandfather whom I had never known. My humiliation melted away.

If further proof of this unworthy deed was needed, leafing through an old notebook concerning family doings of the past some years ago, I came across a photograph of the 30-pounder with some gently mocking lines alongside it: –

He passed an uneventful day
Among the lesser fish:

70

Then met upon his homeward way
A monster on a dish.
He looked upon it with surprise,
And reeling up his line,
Said to himself 'There may be flies
Even more dry than mine.'

It would probably be a mistake for anyone fishing the Fyne these
days to risk fishing the worm, spinner or the white fly. Who
can tell? The present laird may be much less human than was my
grandfather.

Such things usually happen when anglers are young, as Sir Chips
Keswick, the well-known banker and country sportsman, also confessed to me. In his case he received what purists would describe as
his just deserts.

In the 1960s I went every year to fish the Ailort River and Loch
Eilt in western Inverness-shire as a guest of one of the owners.
The loch, which flows into the river and from there into the sea-
loch, was one of the best sea-trout dapping lochs in Scotland, and
nobody got excited unless a sea-trout weighed at least 10 pounds.
The river was dour but charming, without any real holding pools.
One fished the loch and river on alternate days.
   The estate employed a delightful general factotum who,
amongst many duties, would double as ghillie on the tacit
understanding that the rod would leave behind a bottle of whisky
at the end of the day. On the day in question we found ourselves
fishing the river, which was full of running fish. The morning
was as blank as the afternoon. At 5 o'clock my companion was
beginning to fidget and to look somewhat shifty. Wrongly, I
assumed that he wanted to go home. I advised him to do so, being
only 20 and overly polite. But home was not in his mind. He was
trying to save the blank. This was music to me and I asked for his
advice. He looked even more shifty and, with some prodigious
winks, suggested that we should lay aside the rod and try other
tactics.
   We left the pool of non-taking fish and walked the mile to
the sluice, through which the river flows out of the loch. From
a hiding place beside the concrete, my companion produced a
fearsome-looking instrument consisting of a stout ash plant to
which was strapped a foot of fencing wire ending in a large treble
hook. I was then instructed to crouch by the outflow entrance and
give a 'wee rake' along the bottom. I jagged a grilse which, owing
to my incompetence, escaped. My companion then held my hand

and we raked together. At the first touch he turned his wrist, driving the hooks into a sea-trout of considerable proportions. A brief and violent struggle followed – the fish was too big to lift out in one throw – but, just as success seemed imminent, the hook slipped out of the fish and into my thumb over the barb!

Soaked and defeated, we sat on the grass and surveyed the damage. The dilemma soon became obvious – the local doctor was also the local bailiff and the object embedded in my thumb would have landed both of us before the Procurator Fiscal. Clearly we would have to resolve the problem ourselves. Two miles and a lot of pain later, we were in my friend's kitchen and he announced the urgent need for alcohol, which struck me as an excellent start. I produced my bottle of whisky, which he knew would have been his had we landed a fish.

A glass was produced and filled to the brim without water. I was beginning to think that this would be excessive to my requirements but I need not have worried, as it was not for me but for the surgeon. Suitably fortified, he seized my thumb and with a quick slash of his cut-throat razor removed the hooks.

The subsequent visit to the doctor for eight stitches in my thumb passed off with judicial sympathy. I am not sure what the moral of this tale is, except that one should never expect a West Highlander to waste his whisky.

This confession has enabled me to prevail upon my husband to make his own, concerning his first successful encounter with salmon.

While I have been hooked on fishing since boyhood, I had never caught a salmon until the summer of 1950, when I was visiting Edinburgh for a few days to cover a scientific conference for my newspaper. I had taken trout tackle in the hope that I might be able to fish on the Sunday, prior to returning home the following day. The tackle included a very light spinning rod and a fixed-spool reel, a device then beginning to become popular. In addition, I had an extraordinary spinner which I had recently acquired during a visit to Austria, the like of which I have never seen since. It was like a small jewel, a pear-shaped piece of brass about 1 inch long and $1/2$ inch thick, with two wings attached at the thin end and a small treble hook at the thick one. The two sides of the brass were covered with polished mother-of-pearl which flashed in the water. With its weight so concentrated, long casts were very easy, yet the whole thing was elegant enough to have hung from a watch-chain.

I had tried out the spinner with great success on the Hubertsee, a lake belonging to the Krupp family which, as victors in the recent

war, the British could fish as they liked, and was looking forward
to a chance to test it in home waters.

The Edinburgh office of my newspaper put me in touch with
a young man who had access to the Melrose beat of the Tweed,
where he knew the ghillie. He assured me that I would be able to
spin for trout there on the Sunday when, of course, there would
be no salmon fishers. We duly arrived there and I began to fish
with my beautiful spinner when the ghillie arrived on his tour of
the bank. He was friendly and made no comment when he saw me
spinning away. I had no knowledge whatever of salmon rivers, as
the ghillie realised when a salmon showed and I remarked, 'That
was a hell of a trout!' He had just disappeared upstream when I
hooked a fish which my young friend assured me was a salmon.
We duly beached it, and before I could ask what we should do
with it he had hit it on the head with a stone. It weighed in later
at 9 pounds. I was immediately aware that I had committed two
serious legal offences, taking a salmon and doing it on a Sunday.

As I had not taken a fishing bag with me I had brought my
tackle and rubber boots down in the large holdall which was my
only luggage. In a trice the salmon was in the bag, which was then
hidden in the gorse. I fished away and within half an hour hooked
another salmon, which suffered the same fate and also weighed 9
pounds.

When the time came to depart my friend, who was fishless,
instructed me to walk up the river to the point where we had
entered a field leading to the bank while he took off with the
bag towards the road where his car was parked. Nobody saw us.
Thus it was that the first two salmon I ever caught and which
whetted my appetite so much that I was eventually to catch over a
thousand had been poached.

Years later, I learned that my young Scottish friend was teaching
fly casting in the south and that a shooting companion, much
given to practical jokes, was going to him for tuition. As so
much time had passed I could not resist telling my shooting pal
the sorry tale of the Tweed, on the understanding that he would
never reveal his source. Choosing his moment, he artlessly asked
his instructor if he had any tips for poaching salmon. As expected,
the instructor was highly indignant at the suggestion, until he
was accused of having been a salmon poacher in the past. His
confusion at being given the details of his part as a bagman which,
he was told, had come from a third party who had observed the
double crime, was apparently a joy to behold. 'You should always
remember,' he was told, 'that in the country you never know who
is watching you.' It was sound advice.

Others have foul-gaffed a salmon inadvertently, as that ingenious salmon angler and innovator, Richard Waddington, who invented the Waddington fly, confessed to me.

> Just before the Second World War, I was fishing the pool called Ann's Seat on the Monymusk home beat of the River Don in Aberdeenshire. Casting off the north bank I hooked a salmon of about 9 pounds with a fly, a Number 6 Blue Charm as I remember. As I was playing it I noticed another fish, of similar size, following it around as it played. Eventually, because of the nature of the bank, I had to lie on my stomach to get my gaff into the water while holding the rod point up. I struck the gaff home and, to my astonishment the fish on my line continued to pull. I had inadvertently gaffed the companion fish which had been following so closely!
> Having dispatched the fish I then dealt with the other and soon had two salmon on the bank. They looked like siblings and probably were, having hatched together, fed in the sea together and returned together to spawn. A sad end, perhaps. I have not told this story before – not because I was ashamed of it but because I doubted whether anyone would believe it.

My friend Raleigh Place told me of a ghillie on a famous beat of the Spey who accomplished a similar feat recently, but sadly by design rather than accident. After playing a grilse to a standstill the companion fish came a little too near the net and was smartly removed, the hooked fish being netted a few moments later – two for the effort of one.

It seems that in the USA there are odd people prepared to fish foul whoever may be watching, as a shooting friend, Dick Wieser, an American businessman, testified.

> While fishing a large lake in the USA, some friends and I, who have two weeks there every year, were not doing particularly well and became rather suspicious of a stranger who was returning day after day after only a short time with the limit catch of trout in his boat. We quietly asked the water ranger to investigate and he insisted on rowing the suspect's boat the following day. The fisherman seemed unperturbed, and as the ranger rowed him away he realised that, while there was a large net and a bait box in the boat, there was no rod. However, he said nothing and having arrived at the fisherman's chosen spot, which was round a bend out of sight of the other anglers, the ranger dropped anchor. To his astonishment, the angler opened the bait box, withdrew a stick of dynamite, lit it and threw it into the water. Within a few seconds he was scooping up stunned fish with his net.

74

After overcoming his astonishment, the ranger ordered him to stop immediately, began to withdraw the anchor and announced that he would be reporting him for his grave offence. Totally unconcerned, the angler reached into the bait box, lit another stick of dynamite, put it in the ranger's hand and said, 'Now, are we going to fish or are we going back?'

The ranger duly 'fished'.

An intriguing dynamite story came my way when I wrote to Robert Maxwell, the publishing tycoon, shortly before he died in mysterious circumstances while on his yacht. Maxwell's father, who lived in a Jewish settlement near the River Tisza in Czechoslovakia, was in the habit of supplementing his family's meagre diet with carp and other coarse fish caught by various nefarious means. Sometimes he used poison, but he preferred to stun the fish by exploding petrol bombs or sticks of dynamite stolen from nearby salt mines, in which some of the Jews worked. Smaller fish were eaten fresh while the big ones were dried and salted against the days when the river was frozen or in flood.

To celebrate Robert's circumcision, eight days after his birth, his father was required to offer food to a large number of guests and his dynamite fishing for that festive occasion was so successful that he was able to invite half the village!

In his letter to me enclosing the story, and assuring me that it was his only association with fishing, Robert Maxwell hoped that his honesty would excuse his brevity. The comment has raised a few wry smiles among people who knew him, including some *Daily Mirror* pensioners.

My husband once met a poacher who fished for salmon in Scotland in a comparable way, – using hand grenades which he acquired from some army source. He had lost an arm in the process but, continued to poach. There seems to be no end to the eccentricities of those hooked on fishing!

Chapter 9

No Rules

Very early in my angling life the late Sir Thomas Sopwith told me that I would discover that fishing was a sport in which there were no fixed rules, meaning that anything can happen and frequently does. I soon learned that he was absolutely right, especially when I hooked a 'log', hand-lined it in and found it was quite a large salmon. Various stories from several of my informants underscore Sir Thomas's wise observation, like that supplied by Colin Farnell, for example.

> I was fishing a stretch of the upper Kennet which was stocked with both brown and rainbow trout. A good fish rose to my fly and after a considerable battle, with the usual tear-away runs big rainbows make, I eventually landed a 6-pounder in excellent condition. When removing the fly, having administered the last rites with the priest, I was astonished to see that deep in the fish's large mouth, embedded just where the gullet begins, there was a huge sea-hook, two inches long, and a tight coil of heavy line attached to it. Clearly, the trout had taken a poacher's bait – possibly a worm or minnow on a night-line – and had then broken the line which had twisted itself into a tangle, either during the fish's original struggle or subsequently when it tried to swallow it. The fish could not have been too incommoded because it fought extremely hard tearing up and downstream and taking me down to the backing twice.

It is not uncommon to catch a trout lumbered with an artificial fly and a bit of a broken cast – I imagine that most of us have done it – but how this fish could ignore the horrible obstruction in its throat and attempt to feed normally is difficult to explain. It is, however, evidence that a fish does not feel pain and irritation on anything like the scale which higher animals and ourselves would do in such circumstances.

Will a salmon take again once it has been well hooked and lost? There have plenty of examples of salmon caught on fly with another fly already embedded in their mouths, but one that Shirley Deterding caught on the Michaels River, in Labrador, surely settled the question for all time.

Russ, my guide, and I had marked where a big salmon lay under the bank at the end of a pool. Having tried to cover it several times, with the fast water whipping the fly over too rapidly, we waded over to the other bank where, hanging precariously over the water, I managed to roll-cast a fly over the spot and keep it there for a few seconds. At the third try the fish took with an almighty bang and took off downstream, going so fast that Russ had to take the rod and run, with me following as best I could.

The fish eventually slowed down in a deep hole and we managed to retrieve some of the line. After an exciting battle Russ netted a beautiful 15-pounder and, on inspecting it, we saw, to our amazement, that a long length of very thick nylon, about 30 pounds breaking strain, protruded from the mouth with the other end trailing from the vent. We guessed that the fish had taken a baited long-line at sea, had broken loose and the bait with the line had somehow passed through it. The salmon did not seem to be at all incommoded and had still been prepared to take my fly.

Even more remarkable, and possibly unique, is the occurrence reported to me by Sir Seton Wills, the Wiltshire landowner and country sportsman.

In mid-July 1992 I was in a group of anglers visiting Russia to fish for Atlantic salmon in the River Ponoi, on the Kola Peninsula, not far from Murmansk. Our first surprise was the nature of the Ponoi, which I had imagined to be a deep, slow-moving river. Instead, to our delight, we saw a swift river like an oversized River Spey with boulders, eddies and white water – ideal for fly fishing with a long graphite rod and floating line. As all the fish had to be returned, apart from odd ones which we ate, only barbless hooks were permitted. The salmon were very fresh, rose readily and fought ferociously.

One of the party was an American doctor, John Long of Chicago, whose rod was so short that, in order to reach the lies, he needed to fish from a boat. One day he hooked a lively salmon of about 15 pounds – quite large for that river, where there were a lot of grilse – and after a tough fight with many runs it was brought alongside and netted. The ghillie extracted the fly, threw it to one side and held the fish gently in the water until it was sufficiently recovered to swim away slowly – a sight to which we not only became accustomed but came to enjoy.

As the salmon swam beyond the boat it saw the fly which had hooked it dangling in the water and immediately took it savagely, hooking itself. The astonished Dr Long picked up the rod and played the fish again, the salmon having recovered sufficiently to put up another fight. It was duly netted, held again and released.

This time, care was taken to see that the fly was not in the water, although perhaps that was a pity, for a third take would surely have been unique in the annals of fishing.

As it was, the episode raised an interesting question for the Ponoi's records. Should the fish have been entered as one salmon or two? It also suggested that the salmon's memory can be so remarkably short that it is always worth trying again for a fish which has been risen and pricked, even if it has felt the pull of the line. After all, some of the things it devours in the sea, like crustaceans, are quite hard and spiny, and some of them must occasionally escape after administering a bit of a stab.

Even more interesting is the question 'What made the salmon do it?' This incident looks like strong evidence for the theory that salmon take as the result of an uncontrollable reflex triggered off by feelings of angry aggression. My Berkshire neighbour, David Channing-Williams, a telecommunications businessman, reported an event in the same odd category.

As I was fishing the Bucktor pool on the Grenofen beat of the River Walkham, a tributary of the Devonshire Tavy, in October 1985, I noticed the end of a thin hazel stick bobbing in the white water as though the other end was anchored to the bottom. Knowing the local poaching customs, I suspected that the stick might be the end of a makeshift snatching device and, sure enough, when I managed to hook the stick there was a salmon attached to it.

Eventually the salmon tired and came within reach of my wife, who grasped the stick and scrambled up the bank with the salmon flapping vigorously. As I had suspected, there was a rabbit snare attached to the stick and either the poacher had been disturbed or had lost his grip on the implement which he had fashioned on the bank.

The difficult ethical question of whether it was right to keep the salmon never arose because the snare wire broke at its joint with the stick and the fish slithered back into the river. At least the stick with its twist of wire remained in our hands as evidence of our few adrenalin-filled minutes – the only excitement that day – when we recounted the episode to the owners, Philip and Peggy Pawson.

However, the tale was not quite ended. The following day, in a pool less than 200 yards upstream from Bucktor, I hooked a good fish in fast water at the first cast. When landed it weighed just over 9 pounds, including the missing part of the rabbit snare which was still in place round its tail. Its previous unpleasant experiences had not prevented it from having a go at my lure.

The salmon's innately aggressive temperament is surely responsible for the common wisdom that while you cannot bully a trout into taking, you can bully a salmon, as a story provided by Philip Huddy, the distinguished Wiltshire surgeon clearly proves.

> Not many years ago, two friends and I were fishing the Conwy, in North Wales, on a hot, sunny day. There were few fish in the dead low river and they were torpid. However, in the Black Pool, which was quite small, we could see one smallish salmon and for want of something better to do we took turns at dangling a shrimp in front of it. The fish was only about 5 yards from us and, with the help of the obliging current, we soon became so expert that we could actually place the shrimp on the fish's nose and keep it there. I am not exaggerating when I say that we kept this up for more than five hours! For most of the time the salmon did nothing, even when the shrimp was resting on its nose, but occasionally it expressed annoyance and swam round the pool, though always returning to the same place, shrimp or no shrimp.
>
> Just when we were tiring of our attempts to bully it into taking the shrimp, the fish appeared to get really angry and snapped at it, hooking itself and giving my friend, Dr Andrew Chapel, a lively fight.
>
> Although we all reckoned that we had contributed to literally baiting the fish and breaking its resistance we decided that Andrew should keep it. However the salmon was to have the last laugh. Andrew put his prize in his deep-freeze, and while he was away for a few days there was a power cut and it went rotten.

As several of the stories in *Fish Tales* clearly showed, there seems to be no limit to the unpredictable behaviour of the salmon. In one of them Barry Black recorded how, when fishing in Iceland, he had thrown cigarette ends into the water and seen them taken by salmon. Even more astonishing was the titbit inadvertently served up by Stan Wilson of South Africa, also while fishing in Iceland.

> Towards the end of an early July fishing day on the Nordura River, with the sun still shining, though it continued to be cold, I was casting into Rocky Pool, a long run of rapids with big boulders throughout its length. It was 10 pm time to stop, and with my wife, Molly, on the home side of the river, I was persuaded by my ghillie to wade across through the rapids rather than take the boat across, much lower down. Unfortunately, I was not aware that the ghillie had been drinking coffee laced with moonshine – a home-brewed fiery alcohol made out of potatoes.
>
> I was downstream of him, holding tight to his left arm, and we were slowly traversing the frothy, glassy, green river when

we both slipped. In the struggle to keep my balance I lost the detachable patch of sheepskin fastened to my fishing waistcoat along with the dozen flies stuck into it. As it floated away I shouted to Molly to keep an eye on it and all three of us saw the entire patch disappear into the mouth of a huge salmon in the middle of the rapids. That was the last I ever saw of it.

I have heard of a salmon taking two flies – a tail fly and a dropper – but twelve flies is surely a record! A fish to be remembered for ever, even though there had been no contact with it, and a head of the unexpected, rather than a tail. David Gardiner's encounter with a trout offering a difficult challenge is further evidence of unexpected events which can happen at any time.

An old friend who had a regular rod on the Avington beat of the Kennet kindly asked me to fish it one day in late April. It was a glorious morning as I wandered slowly up the right bank, which was beautifully manicured. In one place it was revetted with old railway sleepers, of which the nearest was angled slightly over the river, concentrating the surface flow where, as might be expected, a good fish was lying and rising. It should have been an easy cast but there was an old stake sticking up out of the water, bearing a rusty 6-inch nail.

Having matched my fly as nearly as I could to the one on the water I landed it perfectly alongside the sleepers and a yard above the fish. Unfortunately, as I had half-expected, the line went over the protruding stake and under the nail on it – an inevitable snarl-up should the trout take. It did and I struck, perhaps too early for the fish missed the fly. I was still in with a chance, however, except for one snag. The fly came off the water and hooked itself firmly on the top of a sleeper about 6 inches above the nose of the trout, which was still rising.

I laid my rod down and crawled up the bank until I could reach out to the fly, being particularly careful not to put my fingers over the edge of the sleeper. I managed to release it and backed away from the river. I was standing with my rod, preparing to move downstream, when the trout jumped at the fly which was dangling about a foot above the water. It had well and truly hooked itself and was well and truly landed – a lively 2½-pounder. Did I catch it or did it catch me?

Another of David Gardiner's experiences provided a good example of the no-rules attitude to angling – that, since anything can happen, anything is worth a try on occasion.

We were three cousins fishing in a boat on Chew Valley Lake by the Mendips in the middle of Wimbledon fortnight in 1976. It was, I believe, one of the hottest prolonged periods ever recorded in Britain, and the water was so warm that the lake authorities were having to aerate it by pumping in huge amounts of air through pipes at different places. The air rose to the surface in great, swirling blowholes, and round all of them dozens of trout were rising.

Naturally, all the boats were concentrated round the blowholes but nobody could catch any of the fish. The usual practice, in those days, was to fish with wet flies, and all the favourites were tried in different sizes – Butcher, Peter Ross, Mallard and Claret and so on. When all failed, various unconventional methods were tried and, although nothing comparable could be seen on the water, my cousin, George Holt, put on a tiny Black Gnat and fished it dry. Success was immediate and we followed suit, all catching our limit before lunch. For some reason the fishermen in the other boats did not seek our advice and we departed with the secret.

The question posed by David's 'secret' is whether it would work in similar circumstances another time, for there are certainly no rules about the efficacy of a fly. Time and again, when trout fishing, I have put on a new fly and got a fish right away, thinking, 'Ah! I've got it!', only to find that every other fish ignores it. Then another change of fly quickly produces a rise, but again only one. Very odd!

Of course, it does not serve any useful purpose putting any fly over a fish if the hook is seriously defective. Too many times, especially when salmon fishing, I have failed to examine my fly often enough and suffered the consequences. However, even in those circumstances, there are no firm rules, as Vice-Admiral Sir Hugh Mackenzie recalls.

While fishing the Association water on the Ness a few years after the war, I had already broken the hooks on two flies by hitting the shingle beach behind me when overhead casting. When I was using my third fly, a double-hooked Hairy Mary, Size 8, I thought that I heard it flick on the gravel but, fed up with changing it, I went on fishing. Very soon afterwards I was into a fish which played furiously, jumping all over the place. In due course another angler gaffed it for me and, as he lifted the fish out and I dropped the rod-tip to slacken the line, the fly fell out of its mouth. On examining the fly I realised that both points had been snapped off, barbs and all, just above the bend, yet the two blunt hooks had held somehow. It was a clean-run 12-pound fish and I still have the fly. Good luck or skill in keeping a tight line?

Some of the latter but a great deal of the former, I would say. There are no rules either about the extraordinary rise of salmon which sometimes occurs on Scottish rivers at the darkening – the moment, usually on a summer's evening, when the light just begins to go. After a bright day with little sign of a fish in the water, and still less hope of a take, a pool will suddenly become alive with activity. If one is ready and waiting, a fly put among the fish is near-certain to be taken, and the trick is to land one in time to get another before the magic moment dies away, for the activity rarely lasts more than about a quarter of an hour. Why it should happen on some evenings and not on others remains a complete mystery.

However, the belief that the salmon's sudden arousal is connected with the quality of the light would seem to be supported by James Klootwijk's account of a day on the Thurso river.

The river looked eminently fishable, yet Thursday had arrived and I was still blank. However, there was a change in the weather, with a sky so clear that the high cliffs of Hoy in the Orkney Islands were visible on the northern skyline. I walked to the start of the beat with Morris, my ghillie, then fished down Jamie Sutherland's pool twice without result, one with a floating line, then with a sinking tip. 'Too bright!' Morris commented.

We had covered two miles of the river and eaten our lunch-time piece when Morris remarked dryly that he had never known anybody to catch a fish without his fly in the water. By 3.30 we were nearing the end of the beat at the tiny hamlet of Westerdale, where even the Rock pool proved unproductive. There was just one more – the Manse pool right in the village.

Since lunch, the skies had clouded and dark patches were approaching from the north-east as I started in the Manse. 'A waste of taim,' said Morris, who was getting thirsty. Then, when a mass of dark cloud was overhead, my line tightened. I raised the rod tip and savoured that magic moment, wondering if the fish would stay on. It did and, moments later, Morris tailed a fresh-run 6-pounder. He had never known a fish to take just there but urged me to try the same spot again. With the dark clouds still above, another fish took my Number 6 Shrimp fly immediately, a fresh 5-pounder, which was soon on the bank.

'Get yer fly in the watter quick,' Morris urged, and a 9-pounder took it in exactly the same spot. 'Again!' Morris shouted, his thirst forgotten. I tried once more, but the mass of dark cloud had moved away and I sensed that the river had suddenly gone dead again. Anyway, I had killed enough for one day. It was 4.30 and the pub would be open.

James might just have been lucky to encounter a run of fish going

Carpe diem

through but he suspects, as I do, that the quality of the light had something to do with bringing them on the take, as it probably has during the darkening. Or maybe, according to that great angling innovator, Richard Waddington, the fish simply woke up at the right moment. He believes that they become bored when they are waiting for a rise of water to urge them upstream, and most of them simply go to sleep, as I think I would. After all, as they do not feed, there is not much point in staying awake, and the mechanism which keeps them stationary against the current continues to operate just as our breathing does when are are sleeping.

One of the consequences of there being no rules in fishing is that one never knows what one is going to catch. One can be fishing for salmon or trout and catch a huge pike. Or one can be fishing for pike and catch a record trout. The catch made by John Evans, however, was not only unexpected but most unwelcome, as his friend, Ron Benjamin relates.

> John Evans had turned up to fish in a competition on the Thames at Pangbourne, and was staring at his float, knowing that fish would be hard to catch in the unpromising conditions. He had drawn a peg opposite one of the islands, not the best place to have to sit for five hours with little hope of much memorable action. Well into the competition, his keep-net contained only half a dozen small fish and his float had not moved in the last 25 minutes. He picked up the rod out of its rests and jerked the float forward a few inches, this being a well-known device to induce fish to bite. He tried again, this time with what looked like success. The float slowly slid under the water and he struck, feeling the solid resistance that told him that he was into something big. Whatever it was did not seem to fight much, so he applied pressure and his float appeared above the water. To his horror it was quickly followed by a human hand attached to an arm. With his heart thumping, he decided to keep winding and the body moved into the side, close enough to be seen as that of an elderly man.
>
> Dropping his rod John spent the next few minutes trying to convince his neighbours of the nature of his catch. Eventually the police were called and the match abandoned out of respect.
>
> The poor old chap had been reported missing from a care centre. John does not fish in the Pangbourne area any more.

My husband must be made of sterner stuff. He found the body of a soldier who had been drowned many miles higher up in the River Tees but it was in one of his favourite stretches and he had no qualms about fishing there alone, as he almost always was in those days, before I came along.

Chapter 10

Tales of the Unexpected

While I have never seen an apparition on a river bank, or anywhere else for that matter, there are stories of haunted pools. The trout beat where I fish, at Littlecote, should be a likely venue for an encounter because it is in sight of the ancient house which, a former owner has assured me, has its ghosts. So I live in hope. Meanwhile an angler on the canal nearby gave me this personal experience.

> Many anglers who have fished Redmire Pool, a famous carp fishery a few miles from Ross-on-Wye, believe it to be haunted. Some of us spend all night there in a kind of bivouac, with bite alarms in case we nod off, sometimes several nights in succession. We are in pursuit of monsters, for the lake once yielded a 44-pounder which remained the record for many years. Several of us have experienced a feeling of some other presence there in the mists that rise from the water and there is a story of one angler becoming temporarily unhinged when he believed that something supernatural and horrible tried to squeeze into his bivouac.
> However well or ill founded the story, a priest was prevailed upon to try to exorcise any evil spirits round the lake in the autumn of 1989.

Inevitably – and perhaps disappointingly – in my experience, these strange encounters turn out to have a rational explanation, as Stanley Marber found.

> I was fishing the Duke of Buccleuch's water on the Tweed on a hot day and was resting on the bank, half asleep I suppose, when I saw a very shaggy dog come round a bend of the bank and run towards me. That seemed normal enough but it was followed by another and another until there seemed to be scores of them. Then, when little men appeared, all dressed in blue and carrying long poles, I really began to think that I was seeing things. Of course, it turned out to be the otter hounds, which I had never seen before. They did not do the fishing much good.

I have experienced the odd shock on a river when I have believed that I was alone only to hear someone who had been quietly watching me for quite a while. Usually it has turned out to be another angler anxious to avoid disturbing my fishing, but you never know who is watching you in the country, as Peter Cockwill, a well-known angling writer, fishing instructor, fishery manager and guide on foreign fishing trips, records in this story.

Can you picture the timeless tranquillity of a summer Sunday morning, when the sun has only just begun to warm the air and the breezes have not yet ruffled the surface of the canal, where some 2 inches of red porcupine quill sit jauntily upright waiting to be drawn slowly under as a fat roach takes the bread flake on the hook, some 4 feet below? This was how it was when I was young on the canal at Bude, in North Cornwall, and I was the angler sitting quietly on an old small stool.

Some 20 yards behind me, almost hidden by a stone and earth wall, was the path leading to St Michael's Church. Morning Communion was about to take place and I did not know that my long-time fishing mentor was on his way to that service. He was about to disrupt my peace with a shout of abuse at my absence from church when a better idea occurred to him. Suddenly the lovely red float, so beautifully mirrored by the calm surface, disintegrated as a heavy brick struck it.

Later that day when the friend called round to ask if I had enjoyed any sport I noted the smirk on his face but said nothing, registering the event for retaliation on some future occasion.

In the late autumn I was out with a gun in search of pigeons by the upper reaches of that same canal, and the figure huddled by the bank was instantly recognisable. I began a long and stealthy approach until I could see the smart little red-topped float sitting against reeds on the far bank of the canal. The report of a 12 bore and the instantaneous destruction of the float must have taken several years off that angler's life, but no words were spoken as I took my careful leave, contemplating that everything comes to him who waits.

The trick played on another of my fishing acquaintances, who prefers to remain nameless, was rather more sophisticated.

One morning after breakfast at a lodge on the Dee in Scotland, my host, Raleigh Place, had gone outside into the garden and the housekeeper appeared looking somewhat flustered. 'Major——— wishes to speak with you on the telephone, sir,' she said. There was only one telephone and, knowing that Raleigh was a skilled practical joker, I took comfort in the fact that it was not possible for him to take a telephone call on an extension when one did not

A lesson in Sunday Observance

exist. When I picked up the phone, a voice unknown to me said, 'I am Major——, the Queen Mother's factor at Birchall. I understand that you are collecting material to write a book about the River Dee. The Queen Mother has learned of this and would very much like to meet you and make available to you some of our records, which go back over many years. Would Thursday afternoon be a convenient time? I would suggest 3 o'clock.'

I was suspicious of this conversation but could see no good reason for it to be a hoax, and one had to be polite in case it was not. I pointed out to my caller that I was not writing a book on the Dee but was thinking of writing about some aspects of salmon fishing and would not wish the Queen Mother to be under any misapprehension. My caller replied that the Queen Mother would still like to meet me and hoped that I would accept the invitation. I had to make the appropriate noises and say how delighted I would be.

There was a pause and he added: 'Of course, dress will be informal but the Queen Mother would probably like you to wear a kilt if you could make the necessary arrangements.' This intensified my suspicions, as the request seemed extraordinary. I was then told that he looked forward to seeing me at 3 pm.

I put the telephone down and could see no way in which the call could have been made by Raleigh because the nearest public phone box was 20 minutes away by car, and although my host had a car telephone his Range Rover was outside the front door and I could see that it was unoccupied.

In due course Raleigh reappeared and we set off to the river. On the way I mentioned the telephone conversation and he did not express and surprise about the need for a kilt. He said that he would be only too pleased to help and that if the fishing was no good we could go into Aberdeen that afternoon and make arrangements to hire one.

We duly set out for Aberdeen but when we reached the end of the drive Raleigh said, 'You are a great leg-puller yourself and I couldn't resist the temptation, but I don't think I really want you turning up at Balmoral.'

He then told me how he had done it. He had walked down the drive past the lodge so that I could see him, went round the back, crawled into the Range Rover, lay down and made the call using an assumed voice.

He has never ceased dining out on the coup.

It was a good laugh on a dull fishing day, but I like the contribution from John Roberts of York even more.

We returned to the Tjuonajokk fishing camp after a long day and evening on the River Kaitum in Swedish Lapland. We had caught our fill of grayling up to about 2 pounds, and the cumulative effect of four days' fishing for grayling and arctic charr into the early hours of the morning was taking its toll on our small party. Within the high latitudes of the Arctic Circle the Land of the Midnight Sun gives a 24-hour day for fishing, but creates the problem of knowing when to sleep.

Before we headed off to our cabin, our host invited us for a nightcap in his wigwam-shaped tent, where he promised liberal supplies of alcohol and barbecued reindeer meat. Lying on reindeer skins, gathered round a central fire, two English writers, an American lady, our Swedish host and four Swedish guides settled into a night to remember. Smoke and frying steaks added to the alcoholic haze as, into the early hours, the bottle circulated with stories of fact and fiction about fishing and friends across the world.

It came to the turn of Mikke, our guide, who reminded us of the old Lapp fisherman we had met higher up the river. He lived in an isolated cabin making his living from the grayling and charr he caught. At one time he had had three brothers, who lived the same way and were all bachelors, for no woman would have married into such a spartan environment. Some years ago the eldest brother had died during the winter, when there was no possible access to the nearest town where he should be buried, so the body was taken to an island and buried in the ice until the spring would enable them to take it away by rail to be properly buried in a cemetery.

When spring came, the brothers removed the body, which the ice had preserved, and drove it by sledge across the tundra to the tiny railway station. They knew that the only train which stopped that day was a passenger train, so they had decided to take their brother as a fare-paying passenger, dressed in his best suit and propped up between them in the carriage. If the ticket collector or another passenger got in they would pass him off as asleep or drunk. After a while, as their carriage was otherwise empty, they decided to visit the buffet car for a drink, having forgotten that there was one more stop before their destination. Unfortunately, a passenger boarded the train at that station and entered the compartment with a heavy suitcase. He tried to lift it high on to the rack above the 'sleeping' man, but as the train started with a jolt, the suitcase crashed down on the corpse, slumping it across the seat. Failing to detect a glimmer of life, and fearing he had accidentally killed an old man, he decided to act immediately before his crime could be discovered. He opened the compartment door and threw the body out.

He was just recovering his composure when the two Lapps returned and demanded, 'Where is our brother?' In mounting panic the man replied 'Oh him! He got off at the last stop.'

It is not often that grown men shed tears of laughter but they did that night.

Mikke rounded off the tale by saying that under pressure, when the circumstances were revealed to him, the man confessed what he had done and the corpse was eventually recovered and given a more ceremonious disposal.

A corpse was also involved, tragically, in the story given to me by Roger Sergeant of Basingstoke, as he was fishing for roach in the Kennet just behind our house.

About three years ago, a lot of us turned up to fish in a competition which was to be held on the River Wey at Shalford Park, near Godalming. While most of us were talking about the prospects for the day, which looked good, an official went down to the river to place the pegs in position before we made the draw for places. He saw nothing on his way down, but as he was pegging one spot he saw a human body hanging from a tree. The police were called, and as we were not allowed near the place until full investigations had been made, the competition had to be cancelled. The body turned out to be that of a student from Guildford University.

We were all saddened at the waste of a young life, but we decided that the episode had taught us one lesson – if we ever found a dead body again we would not call the police until the competition was over!

My next story, told to me by Mickey Newlands, a keen Kennet coarse fisher, has a happier flavour, but it could have ended in a triple tragedy in circumstances so horrific that the thought of it makes me squirm.

One summer night two friends and I decided to go to a stretch of the Kennet below Newbury to fish for barbel and anything else that was taking. We were not supposed to fish that water, so it was rather important not to make any noise which might attract the bailiff, who would not have been too pleasant at 1 o'clock in the morning. We had a portable punt about 10 feet long with us, to enable us to anchor in midstream. Our approach to the river was across the canal there and then over some fields. As the punt was heavy, were were pleased to see, in the darkness, a stream which obviously connected the canal with the river, so we put the punt in it, climbed aboard and poled ourselves along. Suddenly we realised that the current had greatly increased, and we were moving at unusual speed. We also realised something else, far more disconcerting; that we were in a concrete drain about 8 feet wide. We must have been 100 yards down the tunnel before we managed to stop the punt by putting our hands on the concrete roof, and then we slowly managed to haul ourselves back up to the tunnel mouth. On the way we realised that we were probably in a feeder tunnel for the Reading sewage system and Lord knows where, or in what, we might have ended up.

In spite of the obvious danger, we were in such fits of laughter as we emerged that we got sucked down again after about 20 yards and had to manhandle ourselves out once more. Since then I have often wondered whether, if there had only been two of us in the punt, we could have made it back. I rather doubt it. It would have been an ignominious end – to be drowned in a sewage system!

One of the others in the punt, Dave Phipps, confirmed the story to me in every detail. In fishing, the hilarious is often not far from the tragic. It would seem to be wise practice, though, to avoid any kind of pipe by a river, whether big or small, as witness the experience of coarse fisherman Martin Porter.

I was fishing in a boat moored in the Thames off Cook's Island above Staines Bridge with my friend Terry, moored by the houseboats there. The chub were giving good sport on trotted maggots, and while I was playing a nice one Terry moved close to net it. He failed to notice a small pipe protruding from one of the houseboats and as he was bending, head down, somebody decided to release their effluent – all over him!

It is odd what people remember best when I ask them for fishing recollections. The most extraordinary memories remain in their minds, some dating back to childhood, like the charming story given to me by a very old gentleman, Mr Pat Ainslie.

In 1911 my parents were staying in Argyllshire and, on arrival, I was presented with a rod already prepared, even down to a worm on a hook, and a ghillie aged 11. There was a burn close by and standing on a bridge I lowered my worm into a pool. No trout took it but an eel did and I heaved it on to the road. Neither of us had any idea how to rescue my one and only hook from the writhing eel but at that moment the stagecoach which ran between Oban and Inverary came by and stopped. A large man descended, put his hand in his pocket, withdrew a sharp penknife, removed the hook, remounted and the coach clattered away.

Few fishermen alive today can have been assisted by the driver of stagecoach. It is a memory from a bygone age.

So long ago that it must be rather like a dream. And where better to meet the unexpected than actually in a dream? I rarely dream about fishing, but my husband frequently wakes up and says, 'I've just had my fishing dream again.' Although the details vary, it is basically the same – he is about to fish a wonderful salmon river but never gets started because he has forgotten or mislaid his rod or night falls before he can start casting.

Any fishing dream is likely to be unsatisfactory. If one lands a monster fish there is inevitable disappointment on awakening. Sometimes, however, the dream action can be so exciting as to be remembered for ever – as Andy Jessett, a former resident of my village, recalled for me.

It was always going to be memorable, whatever happened; my first opportunity to fish the Tweed near Kelso. In spite of several attempts on the Broadlands stretch of the Test, I had not even hooked a salmon, much less put one on the bank, but I was determined that this time it would be different. On the long drive up the A1 to Scotland, Barry, my host, regaled me with tales of the fish he had landed on the beat we were to fish, and I soaked up every item of information about flies and tactics for the high water we were likely to encounter after heavy rains. It turned out to be very high when we saw it, but after visiting the local tackle shop and talking to our ghillie there was hope that it would fall in the night. I could hardly wait to get my head on the pillow with only a few hours' sleep until my big moment.

We were on the bank early and within a few casts I hooked a powerful fish which rapidly took me downstream round the next bend, giving me no option but to follow. It took me right on to the next beat, in fact, where I was somewhat surprised to find that the bank had a hard, paved surface. It was a while before I got things sufficiently under control to take further stock of my surroundings. When I did so I noticed a familiar cathedral on the opposite bank. What was more surprising was the large vessel – more a ship, really – tied up close to where the fight was entering its final stages. I had not realised that they had such ships on the Tweed. It was flattering to see a small knot of spectators who had gathered at the bows to watch the struggle, although, fortunately for my nerves, I did not notice who some of them were until after the fish was safely on the bank.

The caption under the photograph of me holding the fish prepared for me as a memento by Barry, who runs a creative design business, tells it all: 'Salmon, 25 pounds, caught by Mr A. Jessett, 6.55 am on April 1st 1985 on the Winchester High Street beat of the Tweed. The fish was eventually landed next to the Royal Yacht *Britannia*, in full view of His Royal Highness the Duke of Edinburgh. It was fortunate that the fish was landed before Mr Jessett was awakened with his early morning tea and newspaper.'

Unlike many anglers' tales, this one is entirely true, including the date. We were never able to fish that week because of flood conditions, but I had my recompense.

I suppose that when we read about fishing, as you are reading this book, we are fishing vicariously, as Andy Jessett was in his dream. These days we can even do it by watching videos. Another way is to pore over tackle. In fact, I suspect that some people I know never do much else in the fishing line. They collect tackle, especially flies, but never seem to be seen on a river.

Chapter 11

Tales from Distant Venues

The biggest fish I have encountered were the Nile perch of Lake Rudolf, now called Lake Turkana and sometimes the Jade Sea because of its size and colour. I did not manage one bigger than 50 pounds, which is something of a tiddler there, but Shirley Deterding, the Norfolk sportswoman, did rather better with her much wider experience.

> On our many trips to Kenya we usually tried to get up to
> Lake Turkana, a remote and dramatic inland sea stretching into
> Ethiopia. It is exceedingly hot and dry there, the distant mountains
> and surrounding desert making the landscape look lunar, with dry
> winds blowing constantly down the valley. There are two small
> camps on the edge of the lake, one of which still has my record
> Nile perch from back in the 1960s written on the wall. On this
> occasion, however, we flew there in a small plane and landed on
> an island, setting up camp under a thorn bush.
>   Having cleared the crocodiles from the beach we soon began
> catching Nile perch – a prehistoric-looking fish with a big head
> and thick body, and a good fighter for a short time. We returned
> all except what we were going to eat for dinner that night and had
> great fun.
>   On the second day we went round to one end of the island by
> boat, catching fish as we went, and found a huge shoal of tilapia
> with a frenzy of Nile perch feeding on them. We were hooking
> fish at almost every cast when I connected with something
> extremely large. After playing it for several minutes and hoping
> that it was not a crocodile while it literally towed the boat, I
> brought it alongside. It was a Nile perch and the guide judged it
> to weigh several hundred pounds, a new record for me, but I was
> glad to release it. I hope it still resides there.
>   On another trip we were so keen to fish near the Murchison
> Falls on the White Nile in Uganda, where the Nile perch are
> legendary, that we flew there even though Idi Amin's rebels still
> ranged free in the area, killing and plundering at will. Landing
> on a strip where a couple of derelict aircraft lay forlornly on their
> sides, we were eventually approached by a couple of friendly locals

with a small boat, prepared to take us upstream at a price. Soon we were catching fish in the foaming water below the magnificent falls. I hooked one monster which took off downstream and I was fighting it back inch by inch. It stopped dead and then slowly moved away until it took all 200 yards of line, which broke at the reel. A crocodile had seized my fighting fish and taken it slowly back to his lair to devour it – line and all.

Like Shirley, I too visited Murchison Falls at the time when Idi Amin was at his most violent and unpredictable, and our situation was, I think, rather more precarious. We were there as guests of the white Kenyan businessman and politician, Bruce McKenzie, but my husband's passport showed him to be a journalist – a profession which was barred from the country at that time. Idi Amin was in the habit of feeding those he disliked to the crocodiles, which quickly removed all traces, and our safety depended on his friendship with McKenzie, which was so up and down that not long afterwards Amin had him assassinated.

Sir Rex Hunt, the Governor of the Falklands during the war there with Argentina, whom I had the pleasure of meeting while salmon fishing at Kinnaird, told me of his rather different experience with Nile perch in more stable pre-Amin days, when Uganda was 'the pearl of Africa'.

In 1956 or thereabouts, while I was serving as a district commissioner in Uganda, I went fishing for Nile perch from a boat at the foot of the Murchison Falls. I was using an American plug belonging a friend, who had loaned it to me on the understanding that I would be most careful not to lose it because it was a new model and in such demand that it would be difficult to replace. Unfortunately, while I was fishing deep in about 12 feet of water the plug caught on a snag and I could not release it. I looked around and on a sandbar about 100 yards away I could see several large crocodiles sunning themselves. However, I feared my friend's wrath even more than the crocodiles at that stage, so I decided to go down and release it by hand. The chap who was with me in the boat promised to give a sharp tug on the fishing line if the crocodiles moved.

I was almost at the point where the plug was caught up when I felt the line being tugged. My priorities changed in a flash and I thought, 'To hell with the plug!' Nobody ever moved faster to get back into a boat. Once aboard I looked at the sandbar. Not one crocodile remained there. I shall never know whether they had spotted my foolhardy venture, but the only thing that was likely to have moved them was the prospect of a meal.

95

I wonder how many crocodiles are left there. And how many of the elephants and hippos which gave us such pleasure not that many years ago. Sadly, neither Murchison Falls or Lake Turkana, like so many places in Africa, are safe to visit at the time of writing. Another tropical fish I would love to catch because of its legendary fighting power is the mahseer. Sadly, I have never had the opportunity but my former Surrey neighbour, Lilla Rowcliffe, has been more fortunate.

The fishing camp on the Cauvery River in southern India was a most magical place, set on the bank in a glade in the jungle. I had gone there a month before to catch the mighty mahseer which I had read about but never seen. Known to some as the salmon of India, it is an extraordinary fish with huge scales and an enormous mouth. There is one story from the days of the Raj to the effect that one fisherman had a set of playing cards made from the scales of a 90-pound fish. I never got one that size but caught several between 20 and 35 pounds. It was exciting catching such big fish, which fought very hard, but I caught them all on a spinner and it became a fixation with me to get one on a fly. Two years were to go by before I succeeded – with a fish of 35 pounds. When the Muslim guide stripped off and waded in to tail it, my son remarked: 'I wonder if it is less remarkable to catch a mahseer on a fly than to see a Muslim undress in front of a strange woman.'

When I returned to India, the mahseer were being rested and I had the camp to myself, save for the Indian ghillies. I was there to fly fish for carnetic carp which had been so elusive before. I was told that small black flies were best, but they were so rarely successful that I felt there must be something better. My tent was only yards from the river, so from my camp bed I could see deer come down to drink in the early morning, hear elephants in the bush and monkeys chattering in the large banyan tree overhanging the water. I noticed that many fish rose under the tree, usually as a result of something plopping down from the branches. Realising what it was I leapt out of bed and searched my fly-box for a Muddler. The head of the Muddler was round and grey – just like the monkey shit. I only had a large one, but I felt sure that it would do and rushed down to the river in my pyjamas wielding my fly rod. Plop! I had a fish on the first cast and quickly had another. I sat down, confident that I had made a fishing discovery, and the next few days were some of the most rewarding that I can remember.

Standing in the coracle, a large round basket made of reeds and covered in rawhide I was paddled by my guide round outcrops of rocks in the strong current, casting in the eddies and striking as soon as I saw a swirl. I caught 21 carp up to $4^3/4$ pounds – all on my only muddler. In the end only the round, grey head was left but that was what mattered. It was the bit that looked like monkey shit!

Lilla Rowcliffe had cleverly thought things out but my neighbour, Major Anthony Stansfeld, the Managing Director of Pilatus Britten-Norman, the aircraft builders, attributed his wonderful catch almost entirely to good luck.

I have been fortunate to fish from muddy creeks in Borneo, gin-clear Falkland Island streams and the rivers of Darien in Panama, and caught many fish with names I had never heard of. The basic angling principle in such places was usually the same: either one dangled a suitable bait or dragged it through the water, and success depended, at least to some extent, on skill. In general, I am not a great believer in luck when it comes to fishing, the successful are usually the expert fishers. Big game fishing, however, is a different business, because most of the skill lies with the boatman and the luck element plays a larger part. I certainly got more than my fair share of it in the spring of 1993.

I was fortunate enough to be asked out fishing off the island of Mauritius, in the Indian Ocean, while on a business trip there. Most of the morning was spent trolling for bonito to use as bait, which I enjoyed as they ranged from 10 to 20 pounds. After lunch we trolled slowly in the heavy swell, using one live bonito and one dead one from outriggers. My main activity was drinking copious cans of local beer, and I was gently dozing in a reclining chair when distant movement was seen around the area where the bonito were being presented. When the line pinged out of the outrigger I leapt into the playing chair – the crew were more anxious to attach me to the rod rather than to the boat!

I struck as hard as I could and somewhere on the horizon all hell was let loose as a fish, clearly of large proportions, began to emulate a fresh-run sea-trout. After 25 minutes of extreme physical labour I was politely told that it was high time that a fish of that size, estimated at 250 pounds, was alongside the boat. I pulled harder and at last the end of the 40-foot trace appeared. In a large wave I caught a glimpse of a vast blue fish which did not like what it saw and promptly took out every yard of line I had laboriously pumped in over the previous hour. It did this by sounding vertically downwards for 1000 feet or so. The next hour was more like marathon running or some other masochistic sport. I was constantly pumping up the fish, often losing 2 feet for every yard gained. Eventually the fish came alongside and was lassoed and dragged inboard – a 700-pound blue marlin about 12 feet long. I would willingly have let it go but it was obviously vital to the crew that it should be kept, as much for the meat as for the local kudos.

It was a tremendous thrill, but it was accompanied by the uncomfortable thought that I will never catch a bigger fish and that certain divorce would ensue if I had even part of it stuffed. I settled for the fish's bill as a souvenir and have set it up on a plinth in our house.

The bill is certainly impressive, and Anthony need not be despondent about having captured his ultimate fish. Size is not everything and, in any case, he might catch an even bigger marlin should he ever return to Mauritius. When I was there, sadly out of the marlin season, there was one which had weighed 1100 pounds mounted in its entirety on the wall of the hotel!

Our old friend, Bernard Venables, the well-known angler, artist and writer, who was once a colleague of my husband's on the *Daily Express*, searched out a foreign monster which I and, I would guess, most anglers had never even heard of.

I was in the Zambesi Valley in Zambia, in country which is largely uninhabited because of the tsetse fly. Staying with me in a Game Department camp was John Kabemba of the Bembi tribe. Having heard so much about the huge vundu, a giant form of catfish to be found in the river, I asked to be guided to a good spot in the hope of experiencing the vast run which, I had been told, the vundu makes with enough power to break an 80-pound line like thread. I was taken to the tail of an island where hippo were lolling and blowing about 300 yards out. Between us the water was seething with tiger fish and, I was assured, vundu. I had brought some of the steak, intended for us, as bait, but it was invariably taken by tiger fish which bit through the nylon so that I was soon without any big hooks.

'That's it then,' I said to John. 'No more hooks!'

'Search in your bag,' he said. 'You must have a hook there somewhere.'

I searched and found a tiny threadline spinner on a short length of 7-pound breaking strain wire. To humour John I detached the hook and put a small piece of steak on one of the prongs of the tiny triangle. I had 300 yards of line on the reel, but the bait was too light to cast more than a few feet from the bank.

After a few minutes the line began to run, steadily stealing away. It ran and ran until I knew it had reached the place near the hippos. Then it stopped. I applied the gentlest pressure and it began to come as I wound very slowly.

'Do you know how to use a gaff, John?' I asked.

'What is a gaff, my friend?'

I explained and added, 'If I should manage to get this fish to the bank, hold the gaff over its back and pull the point in. Whatever you do, don't make a swipe with it.'

Wild hopes began to rise as the fish kept coming. Suddenly I could see the great broad ugly head with tiny eyes and huge whiskers.

'Are you ready, John? Remember what I said.'

Behind me the gaff came down in a violent arc. There was a huge thrash, a hiss and a heave and there on the bank was the vundu – all 100 pounds of it.

John put his hand on my shoulder. 'With a vundu you must always strike hard, my friend.'

More and more anglers are taking advantage of the still unspoiled Atlantic salmon rivers being opened up by the Russians, especially in the Kola peninsular. As this area includes the port of Murmansk, a major naval base, it was a closed military zone in the Soviet era, out of bounds, to most Russians as well as foreigners, and the salmon were never touched. So the stocks of fish are as they must have been in Scotland and many of the English rivers centuries ago. His Grace the Duke of Wellington, one of the keenest fishers I have encountered, was among the first to sample it and sent me this mouth-watering report.

Towards the end of June 1992 a friend, Mike Savage, and I joined an American group to fish the Ponoi River on the Kola Peninsula, which is within the Arctic Circle of north-west Russia. Frontiers, an American sporting agency, obtained a lease on the whole Ponoi river system and set up a camp about 40 miles upstream from the mouth, where it joins the Barents Sea. We arrived on the evening of 27 June after a long and tiresome journey, of which the fourth and last leg was by helicopter. There followed six days of excellent fishing, of which one will remain with me as uniquely memorable. The Ponoi system is huge, the main river being over 300 miles long with numerous tributaries. Much of this water is unknown territory and very little has been fished with a fly although nomadic Lapps take a few by nefarious means and bears catch some spawning fish.

On 1 July Mike and I were asked to explore and report on the middle reaches of the Panorche river, one of the Ponoi's most important tributaries. Using a helicopter like a taxi, and with a Russian guide as well as a pilot, we flew about 30 miles upstream and then descended to take a closer look at the river, following every twist and turn as it wound its way through thick wooded banks. Branches of trees slipped past, appearing almost to touch the tips of the rotor blades.

Some 40 miles upstream we found a group of four likely-looking pools all fairly close together, and we landed on a beach covered with large boulders. After our pilot eased the machine down gently, like a duck on to eggs, we went our separate ways with the guide, Dimitri, flitting between us. The river was about the width of the middle Spey and had all the characteristics of an ideal Highland stream. The water was very clear and slightly peat-stained, and the wooded banks, quite steep in places, sloped down to the rocky stream bed. In Scotland the valleys would have had sheep and cattle grazing, but here there was no sign of man and his animals and the grass was full of wild flowers. The woods, mostly birch and spruce, were carpeted with plants like bilberry and a mass of pink flowers which, I learned later in the Helsinki Botanical Gardens, were a cloudberry. Dimitri told me that in the autumn there is a profusion of berries on which the bears gorge themselves before hibernation.

My first pool was about 40 yards long and 20 yards wide. It was on a bend with a rock face on the far side. Within minutes of stepping into the pool I saw a fish show under the rock face. He took the fly at the first cast and after a hard fight I beached a fresh fish of about 8 pounds which I released. Subsequently I took two more fish from this pool and lost two, one of which put up a particularly spectacular fight. He took the fly on the lip of the pool and, after charging round, much of the time in the air, he decided to leave the pool and go downstream. This meant following him through 100 yards of rough water. Luckily, Dimitri saw my plight from afar and he came racing downstream after me. We soon found that my fish had managed to snag the line on a broken bough of willow, but Dimitri freed it. Off went the fish again, only to get round a large rock. Again, Dimitri nobly waded in and freed the line, only to have the fish go down again and once more wrap himself round a rock. This time it was too much even for my 15-pound breaking strain cast and I was broken. A pity! He looked a fish of more than that weight, although of course I would have put him back under the mandatory catch-and-release policy.

After this encounter, I decided to try the pool downstream. At the bottom of the rough water the river opened into a long, slow pool where it crossed an open valley, but there was a nice-looking neck and as I approached it I saw a fish show about 15 yards below the bottom of the rough water. I caught that fish and another which showed slightly lower down. I also lost two others which threw the hook after several minutes of acrobatic display.

It was now lunch time and I could look back on a pretty good morning – five fish to the bank and four lost. Losing so many with barbless hooks was inevitable.

I walked back upstream to join Mike, who had also had a good morning with about the same number of fish hooked. In comparing notes we found that we had hooked every single fish we had seen show, as well as quite a few others. While Dimitri and the pilot identified the pools on the map and compiled notes of our fishing, Mike and I took enormous satisfaction in being the first people ever to take salmon on a fly from those four pools.

Before we left that place I made my own little exploration of the area. Of birds there were none to speak of, save for a few white wagtails, a variant of our pied species. As everywhere else on the Ponoi there were cuckoos calling all the time and I could not help wondering what unfortunate birds were acting as surrogate mothers for all those little ones. The whole area was covered with a small shrub with pink bell-like flowers which I had not seen before. I nurtured a small bit of it all the way home in the hope that my wife would identify it. She did, it was bog rosemary. My most exciting discovery was the fresh tracks of a bear, almost 6 inches across.

When it was time to get started again Mike and I made a serious error. We decided to go 10 miles downstream, where we had seen some nice pools. We fished four of them and hooked only four fish, of which we landed two. We should have gone upstream with the shoal which we had found in the morning. Nevertheless, we had hooked over 20 fish between us and landed 14 – and on water never fished before.

There was one more pleasure to come. On the way back directly over the tundra, standing alone and majestic by a small lake stood two bull moose.

I understand that further north still in Russia there are unfished rivers with runs of huge salmon like Norway's best before they became netted out. Let us hope they will not be over-exploited in Russia's rush for foreign currency.

In my first book, some of my contributors wrote about the big sea-trout which can be caught in the Falkland Islands. Another island as far away, which is just as productive and maybe more so, is Tierra del Fuego – the Land of Fire – at the southern tip of South America, where Charles Darwin reported seeing fierce and primitive savages.

Robert Rattray, who travels far and wide to fish, reports.

In 1975, while in the United States, I read a book by an American angler called Joe Brooks who had visited Tierra del Fuego in

Fishing the wilderness

the 1950s and caught sea-trout wighing up to 20 pounds on fly. They were the offspring of ordinary brown trout which had been introduced into the rivers there and had developed the habits of running to the sea to feed and, of course, had to return to the rivers to spawn. I decided that I would get there if I could, and did so in 1991 with three companions. There is one big river, inevitably called the Rio Grande, which is like a huge counterpart of the River Spey, but there are some much more attractive smaller ones and it was two of those, called the Ewan and the Irrigoyen, which we fished.

I should point out to anyone with a mind to go that it is essential to have everything fixed up first. Fishing is fairly free for all, but the owners of the huge sheep *estancias* organise things so that, without their agreement and assistance, access can be extremely difficult. To fish the Irrigoyen we had a six-hour drive in a four-wheel-drive vehicle over rough terrain and then a three-hour walk!

The Ewan is like a very deep River Test and one fishes in the tidal area, for the fish spawn only about 4 miles upstream. In addition to sea-trout there are brook trout. The sea-trout go to 30 pounds but the biggest we got weighed 14. They were tremendous fighters, jumping all the time like no others I have ever seen. They are also a wonderful-looking fish; deep and fat, and many of them heavily spotted, like a river brownie. The custom is to fish with single-handed trout rods and a biggish fly like a Maribou Muddler. One also wades in many places so you can imagine what happens when a big one takes off – everything! Catches of up to 100 pounds per rod in one day are not uncommon, but nearly all the fish are released, hopefully to spawn, which is only right because I suspect that some of them are very old as there seems to be very little natural predation.

I hope to go back again – so long as I stay fit enough. Apart from the inaccessibility it can be very windy and very wet.

The story given to me by Dr Leonard Selby, who now practises in London but once worked at a hospital in Stellenbosch, not far from Cape Town, South Africa, is certainly offbeat enough to qualify as a 'tail' of the unexpected, had the recipients of the catch known about it.

I was a keen sea fisherman and about once a month during the season I would manage to catch one or two big tuna in the 160-pound class. While the tuna were delicious to eat,they were difficult to carve up properly because of their size. So I worked out a deal with an expert dissector of such large bodies – the technican in charge of the hospital mortuary, who also had refrigeration facilities.

I would place the tuna on one of his marble slabs and eventually receive all the prime cuts I needed. The rest went to him and to friends who, I trust, never gave any thought to the usual function of the cutting instruments he used.

Dame Shirley Porter, whose father founded Tesco, and who has achieved her own distinction in local government, was spared the problem of cutting up the monster she played with such patience.

We were staying at the Rod and Gun Club in the heart of the Everglades, in Florida, enjoying a day out fishing in a boat about 50 feet long. All morning I had managed to hook only catfish, which I threw straight back, so you can imagine my delight when I suddenly felt a really strong tug on the line. The rod curved in a semicircle until I thought it was going to snap, while I tried to reel in and stay inboard, determined that the monster on the other end of the line was going to be mine.

The skipper hurried over to give me a hand, saying, 'You've got yourself a real big one, this time. Take it easy and bring him in slowly.' But it seemed that the fish had mammoth strength for, try as I might, I could not reel in any line and it was pulling so viciously that I was being hauled off my chair. Even the skipper began to look worried.

A shout from the stern of the boat told us that someone at that end was also into a monster hooked at the same time as mine and giving the same problems. Yes – you have guessed it – we had caught our hooks under the boat and were playing each other!

Chapter 12

Of Nets and Other Paraphernalia

We have all been thankful for landing nets, especially when caught up a tree or in the reeds, for it is surprising how easily a tightly caught fly can be safely bashed off by an expertly wielded net. But what a bore they are to carry around! They catch on everything and a salmon net is particularly difficult to carry and handle especially when one is on one's own. I do not like plunging a gaff into a salmon so whenever possible I beach my fish.

I have disliked salmon nets since my first experience of seeing one in action. It was the first day of an early spring fishing expedition with my husband, before we were married, on the Clohamon beat of the River Slaney, in Ireland. He had hooked a salmon of about 17 pounds on a wooden minnow and played it to a standstill, drawing it towards a net held by an Irish ghillie who, it turned out, had very little experience. I had never seen such a fish and was most impressed, remarking, 'You've caught a whale!'

'Not yet,' he answered, grimly, while eyeing the ghillie with deep suspicion. Sure enough, the ghillie made a hash of it, lifting the net too soon, before the salmon was really in it. The meshes tangled in the treble hooks of the bait and, with its head still outside the net, the fish shook itself free and swam away. Harry's response revealed a verbally violent side of his nature which I had never seen before – although I would see it again on occasion.

I reckon that I behaved in a more rational, if somewhat undignified, manner in not dissimilar circumstances while fishing in Norway. I sat on an even larger salmon which had slipped the hook in shallow water during my first attempt at beaching. I was quite alone on my side but someone fishing on the opposite bank applauded my efforts, clumsy and unorthodox as they were, as I gave the fish the *coup de grâce* with a stone, while still astride it, and scooped it on to the shingle.

Although I was wet, I was, of course, rather fortunate compared with Sir Robert Atkinson, an engineer and businessman of Itchen Abbas, in Hampshire, who kindly sent me his Norwegian recollection.

Salmon fishing is my chief hobby and in 1973, while fishing in Norway near Trondheim, I hooked a large fish which took me up and down the bank. Ultimately, I played it out and brought it into the side where it was not possible to beach it. My friend, in the distance, who was totally inexperienced, had seen the action and came running to my assistance with his gaff. He missed the fish in the most ridiculous way, so I told him to get my net which, under my detailed instructions, he managed to wield effectively, landing a beautiful salmon of at least 25 pounds. As it had otherwise been a barren day, I was delighted, but rather prematurely.

The awful man rushed up the steep bank with the fish in the net and threw them both down so that he could dash for his whisky bottle to celebrate. The fish jumped clear of the net and of the hook and started flopping down to the water. I dashed after it but slipped on a rock and fell on my rod, breaking the tip. By now the fish was by the water and I slipped again – this time into the river, splitting my knuckles badly and smashing my watch. Ignoring all this, the salmon entered the river gently and swam away.

Being the perfect gentleman, I scrambled ashore, dripping wet, saying, 'Well dash it all!' though in rather stronger language. My simmering anger with my friend was slightly assuaged when I noticed that, in all the excitement, he had knocked over his bottle of whisky, losing the lot and being deeply shocked about it.

I never fished with him again.

Ghillies, of course, witness many netting disasters which, on rare occasion, they can rectify, as George Johnson, a former head ghillie on the Wye told me.

One of my fishermen hooked a small grilse and when he tried to land it with his 3-inch mesh net it went straight through. Another rod came along and the fish did exactly the same with his net. So there it was – through two nets with the fishermen hanging on to the handles. Fortunately, I happened to arrive on this rather farcical scene, saw the situation and, stretching my net taut, got behind the fish and threw it on to the bank with a flick. A canoeist who was passing, as unfortunately they so often are these days, called out, 'I've never seen a ghillie playing tennis before!

In *Fish Tales* I told a story of a salmon which obligingly jumped into a landing net being held in the air. Pat Ainslie of Aynhoe Park, near Banbury, told me of a somewhat similar experience.

In 1989, at the age of 84, I was fishing the Brora and happened to be alone when I hooked a large salmon. While I was playing it, the middle joint of my old 11-foot split-cane rod snapped and there I was holding two bits in my left hand while my right hand tried to operate the reel, as well as holding my net. Fortunately I was

With a little help from a friend

standing on a wide ledge about a foot above the water which was only a foot deep there.

While I was wondering how I would cope the fish, which had been very active, suddenly decided to swim quietly towards me. I put the net into the water and it swam straight into it! It was a fresh fish weighing 20^1/$_2$ pounds and was 44 inches long. How lucky can one be?

My American friend Ted Allaman would have been just as grateful for a net.

I was fishing with a friend in Iceland, who wanted to show me how to use a tailer to land a salmon, something I had never tried before. He hooked what he thought was a small salmon and gave the rod to me while he went along the bank to get the tailer. Within a few moments I realised that the salmon which had shown itself was not the fish I had on. The real fish was, in fact, the largest salmon I had ever seen. My friend insisted that I should continue to do battle and I fought it for an hour, finally bringing it alongside to be tailed. Regrettably, instead of being about his business my companion was so interested in looking through the gin-clear water at the fish, which had prominent net marks and a seal mark, that he missed a good chance to tail it. As a result, the fish made another run and dislodged the hook, much to my annoyance, although there was not much I could say, as it had been his fish.

After the salmon had rested from its almost fatal struggle down at the end of the pool it moved upstream and jumped four times out of the water in what looked like a derisive fashion. I had never seen a fish put its fingers to its nose before but I am sure that one did.

Bob Morris, a specialist tackle dealer of Darenth in Kent, was luckier but might easily have lost a record fish, of which he is justifiably proud, because of net trouble.

Towards the end of January I was fishing for barbel on a stretch of the River Medway which is quite narrow and where, in fact, there are not all that many barbel. One can fish there the whole season and be lucky to hook two, although I knew that one fish of 14 pounds 13 ounces taken there had established a new British record and had been safely returned to the water. However, I was not fishing for that specially but for any old barbel. The weather was terrible, with a gale-force wind and driving rain, so it was no wonder that I was quite alone. Using a 12-foot carbon rod and ledgering with a blob of paste of the kind I also use for carp, I had nothing except a few taps from chub but around 6.30 pm, when it was pretty dark, I saw a big fish roll in the swim. I put the bait over it and 10 minutes later it took it.

During a hard fight which lasted 15 minutes, I accidentally knocked my landing net into the water and saw it being carried away by the current. There was nowhere I could beach the fish so, with nobody in earshot, I was reduced to getting it out by hand. I managed to grab it and then had further difficulty taking it up a steep, slippery bank to be weighed and photographed because, of course, there was no way that I could kill it. It was so big that I thought it might be a new record and once I had weighed it I knew it was – 15 pounds 7 ounces. When I studied my photographs I had no doubt that it was the same barbel which had established the previous record and had put on some more weight since being returned. Fortunately, I managed to call some witnesses on my mobile telephone so that there could be no doubts and the fish has since been accepted by the British Record Fish Committee.

I suppose somebody else may catch it again one day when it is even bigger, but nobody had done so by the time the season had ended in March 1993. I even managed to get my net back, weeks later, when somebody fished it out.

There are, of course, nets and nets, and those I most dislike are the ones left by poachers, some of whom operate with astonishing audacity, probably relying on the excessive good nature of magistrates who do not regard poaching as theft. My husband and I frequently stayed at a hotel overlooking the Aberdeenshire Dee where the main salmon pool could be plainly seen from the dining-room window, providing interest at all times because there were usually fish showing in it. One evening one of the guests hooked an obstruction with his fly and it turned out to be a rope tied to a large net. Poachers must have set the net at night right in front of the hotel.

In view of the scarcity of salmon for the angler these days, I confess that I was not too upset by the grim episode described to me by George Johnson.

When I was Head Ghillie on the Cadora beat of the Wye, I went to my boat early one morning and found the police and an ambulance there. 'What's up?' I asked and the police explained that they wanted to use the boat because they believed there was a body in the water and were hoping that it was a well-known poacher who had given them a lot of trouble. They found it and, sure enough, it was. Working alone, the man had been dragging the pool, having pegged nets in under the water on the previous evening. When he had started pulling a net out in the darkness it had wrapped round his body and drowned him.

Only three days later, his son was caught doing the same thing. Such is the attraction and the possible rewards of poaching the king of fish.

The damage which poachers inflict with their nets is minor compared with the nets I hate most – the commercial salmon nets used in the sea and in the estuaries of some of the Scottish rivers, like the Tay. At one stage recently, there were 32 netting stations on the Tay which those salmon which had survived all the hazards of the sea had to face. Their annual toll was appalling and, on a visit there in 1991, I learned why. Every year from 5 February until 20 August, night and day except for weekends, boatmen were operating nets from bank to bank in such a way that for any fish to get through was almost impossible. I had always believed that, when netting across the river, they were required by law to leave a clear channel, one third of the river's width, to give a proportion of the fish a chance. Not so.

When netting started, many years ago, it was done by manpower, rowing boats and heavy hempen nets which limited the number of sweeps that could be made in a day or night. Now it is done by motor-boats using nylon nets and engines to do the hauling, so that two men can make 30 sweeps or more each shift. No wonder there were so few fish for anglers and that the whole Tay system with its many tributaries and great loch, which once formed the greatest salmon resource in Europe, was in such tragic decline.

It was my good fortune to meet the two men who deserve most credit for reducing this carnage and hopefully, in time, ending it – Michael Smith, who owned the Dalguise beat of the Tay and his father, Sir Alan Smith, a businessman who, while not being an angler, was greatly disturbed by the general effects which the lack of salmon was having on the Scottish economy. A salmon caught in a net may be worth little more than £1 per pound, but a rod-caught salmon is worth far more because of the spin-off to the hotels, the shops and the garages where visiting anglers spend money, apart from the ghillies and others involved in the fisheries. Michael Smith had been agitating for the removal of the most damaging nets for years, but the riparian owners who would have to find the money to buy them off were being too slow in getting their act together. Finally, when time was running out, the diplomatic Sir Alan was called in to knock their heads together. Officially the co-ordinator of the appeal fund, he insisted that everything had to be completed within three months, on the principle that this would concentrate the minds of those responsible. Sure enough, it did. The nine most damaging netting stations were bought off and it is hoped that the rest which are still operating in the estuary will be removed by the end of the decade so that this great river will start the new century entirely free from netting.

Apart from his oustanding business skills I feel sure that Sir Alan's charm had much to do with his success. It would seem that he was destined for success because he told me an extaordinary story of how, as quite a poor boy, he had been with his mother when her fortune was being told. The fortune teller, a woman, took his hand and told them that one day he would go to Buckingham Palace. After a few more words she said he would then go to the Palace again, which seemed even more unlikely. Finally she pronounced that he would go there a third time. She was proved right. He went twice to receive two DFCs won during his war service with the RAF and then, forty years later, for his knighthood for services for the Scottish textile industry. One meets some wonderful people through fishing!

While I have been fortunate enough to hook a few salmon while fishing from boats, I much prefer to wade or fish from the bank. There is too much paraphernalia in a boat for my taste, nets being part of it. If we are anchored, as happens on the Spey, where the ghillies let the boat down the stream a few yards at a time on a long rope, I am always scared of fouling the rope if I hook a fish, or even the anchor. It has not happened yet, but Ron Benjamin, my local tackle dealer, recalled a memorable encounter with an anchor.

The trip out on *Wayfarer II* had been uneventful as Tony, the skipper, dropped anchor about three miles off the Needles. The fishing was fast and furious with skate, conger and pollack being caught by all the rods. With two hours of the trip remaining, the sky began to darken and the wind picked up, beginning to blow really hard. Tony decided that we could fish for a further hour but would then have to head inshore to calmer water. We continued to fish, but Tony decided that we had better be off and as we stowed our rods away he switched on the electric winch to pull up the anchor. It soon started to labour, and it was clear that the anchor was stuck fast to the sea bed, so we all grasped the rope and heaved. Suddenly it began to move, but still against great resistance. Very slowly, with the winch labouring and starting to smoke, the rope was wound on to the drum and the anchor appeared. Attached to it, as we stared in amazement, was the Isle of Wight telephone cable!

Bernard Aldrich remarked casually that the time had come to start collecting corks for his home-made wine. 'I would like you, Steve, to keep watch on the cork tree to see when they are ready' he said, without a smile. 'It should be fruiting soon.'

Such was my awe of Bernard then that I took him seriously. I kept looking up at the tree for bunches of corks until the smiles all round made me realise that I was being spoofed.'

The ritual dram of whisky on the river is the usual association between drink and fishing, but a rather unusual aspect of it was recalled by my friend and neighbour, Richard Astor.

My late father was fishing the Spey, where he owned a beat, when the river was in such heavy spate that the rods caught no fish during the whole of the week. They did, however, make a most unusual catch with their spinners. Several empty whisky barrels lapped out by the torrent from a famous distillery 1/2 mile upstream came floating by and, having nothing better to do, the rods managed to hook several and draw them into the side. They were urged on by the ghillie, a Speysider who knew exactly what to do with them.

Back in his hut he boiled a few pints of water and swished it around in one of the barrels, thereby drawing out the whisky which had soaked into the wood. He managed to fill several bottles with drinkable Scotch and was preparing to extract more when the distraught distillery manager descended in search of his property.

While I have experienced alcoholic ghillies, some so bad that their lairds have forbidden me to offer them a drink, I am surprised these days, how many decline the ritual dram when offered it after a salmon has been landed. But the old legends persist. According to Bob Grant of Kinnaird beat, when Tay ghillies are offered a dram they always insist on using water straight from the river to dilute it. The explanation is that when the first fishing boat enters Loch Tay on the opening day of the season, a bottle of whisky is broken over the bow in an ancient ritual.

Diluting whisky at all is regarded by many ghillies as sacrilege, as Vice-Admiral Sir Hugh Mackenzie, long known to all his friends as Rufus, recalls.

My father, who was a doctor as well as a keen salmon fisher, disapproved of strong drink on medical grounds. One day, after landing a nice fish on the Spey, he offered his ghillie the customary dram, poured it out of his flask and, in accordance with his views started to add water to it. Appalled by what he was seeing and knowing my father's concern for anyone's health he cleverly intervened with: 'Careful with the wachter, Dochtor. It maks me terrible seek!'

Michael Smith, the owner of the Farleyer fishery on the Tay, offers an explanation of why ghillies stopped wearing the fore-and-aft deerstalker hats which were once popular. On a very cold and windy day one of them had the ear flaps loose and fastened under the chin when a rod asked him if he would like a dram. The ghillie could not hear him, missed the dram and news of that tragedy quickly spread down the river.

Michael also supplied my favourite drinking ghillie story, insisting that it is true.

> A head ghillie on the Castle Grant beat of the Spey called Eric Robb was a big drinker who died in his early fifties, apparently not to his surprise. He left instructions that the inscription on his headstone should read; 'If whisky be the water of life what the hell am I doing down here?' His wish was duly observed, although the Minister insisted on removing the world 'hell'.

That old ghillie clearly had a sense of humour and, while the odd one can be unbelievably dour, most of them enjoy a good laugh and are prepared to provide one. While fishing the Kinnaird beat of the River Tay, I was astonished to hear the chief ghillie, Bob Grant, remark that the first three fish taken on the beat in the 1990 season had been caught by the balls. He then explained that they had been caught by two regular rods called Dr and Mrs Ball.

The fish book showed that his story was true, as was Bob's account of the strange behaviour of an ageing playboy whose romances had once helped to fill the gossip columns. When fishing the Spey, the gentleman had fairly frequent recourse to the riverside bushes and Bob noticed that whenever he did so he first removed his cap. Finally unable to control his curiosity Bob asked for an explanation for this odd behaviour. With a weary smile the angler observed: 'One must always show respect for the dead!'

Occasionally ghillies need a sense of humour when the joke is on them. When Bob Grant was a ghillie on the Spey, a certain Major Miller was a regular rod. Although he had an artificial leg from a war injury, he insisted on wading and always managed, even on a boulder-strewn bottom. The only time he needed assistance was with the removal of his waders at the end of the day. The first time Bob helped with this task, he had extricated the sound limb and was pulling hard on the other when he suddenly found himself on his back with the waders, artificial leg and all. The major had undone the straps holding the leg to his body and this turned out to be his regular joke on ghillies at their first encounter.

One of the pleasures of fishing is in the diversity of ghillies one meets and the converse is, presumably, true. On most beats ghillies encounter such a wide range of personalities over the years that they need to be diplomats, especially in these days when so many are paying rods. Their diplomacy is often expressed by their silence, which is nowhere so eloquent as on a salmon river when a rod has muffed an opportunity to add another fish to the catch record that is so important both to the ghillie and the owner. However, I have never met one quite as diplomatic as the Itchen ghillie described to me by Dermot Wilson.

A certain Lord Chief Justice used to fish a stretch of the Itchen which I knew well. The stretch had the rare distinction of being looked after by a man who was acknowledged as the most tactful keeper in the whole of Hampshire. He was also one of the best.

One day this exemplary keeper, whom I shall call Isaacs, happened to come across the Lord Chief Justice when flies were hatching and trout were rising all round him. The judge had caught nothing and had lost enough of his judicial equilibrium to complain bitterly. 'There's just not much of a rise on today, is there Isaacs?' he said trying to rationalise his failure.

It was a full two minutes before Isaacs replied. As he watched the dimples and swirls on every side he cudgelled his brain for an answer both true and tactful. 'Not at your lordship's fly, sir,' he eventually replied.

Some ghillies, of course, are rather better known for their forthright lack of tact, especially if a particularly welcome opportunity arises. Bob Grant, who has long been convinced, as I am, that the major cause of the Tay's decline is greedy commercial netting, could not resist an occasion when one of his guests was a prominent landed lord who was also a rapacious netsman.

'I think that there should be no closed season for netsmen,' Bob observed.

'What makes you say that?' the noble angler asked, brightening at the prospect.

'Because I think that we should be allowed to shoot the buggers at any time!'

Katriona Christie's experience was less direct but somewhat chastening.

My father, an admiral who was a keen salmon fisher, taught me to cast by practising on our tennis court, which he could see out of his study window. Having set up a saucer 20 yards or so away, he showed me how to put a fly into it and left me to get on with it. I was only 17 and soon got bored but, being a tough disciplinarian, he would lean out of the window and make me continue.

The day came when he took me down to a beat on the Wye, below Ross-on-Wye, to put my lessons into action. 'Now you can really practise your casting,' he said, putting me into a pool which, in the circumstances, was probably one of the least promising. Both he and the ghillie disappeared and, miraculously, it was not long before I hooked the only fish of the day. Clearly my practice had paid off but, unfortunately, my father had not told me how to play a fish, no doubt convinced that I would not get one. By the time they heard my cries, my arms were like lead, my back was aching and I felt so exhausted that I asked one of them to take the rod. They refused and said that having started the job I had to finish it. By the time I did so I had been playing the fish – a fresh-run 13-pounder – for 45 minutes!

One might have expected congratulations but all the ghillie said was. 'Admiral, I thought your daughter was going to expire before the fish.'

Ghillies nearly always complain to me that I am not fighting the fish hard enough and should give it more strain, but salmon are scarce enough without losing them. I may take time in getting them in but I have lost very few and I suspect that when I have done so it was because I was giving them too much stick.

Inevitably, however, there are times when, with the best will in the world, a ghillie has to exert his rightful authority as guardian of the beat over some transgressing rod. Bob Grant's brother-in-law, who ghillied on the Spey at Pitchroy, was with a Frenchman who caught a salmon of about 10 pounds on a fly. He tailed it and was about to hit it on the head when he found himself pushed roughly aside by the Frenchman, who replaced the hook, firmly as he thought, in the scissors and put the salmon back with the intention of playing it again. The ghillie thought this grossly unfair and said so, being scarely able to forbear to cheer as the fish shed the hook and escaped.

Bob tells a similar story about a Luxembourgeois who was fishing the Spey at Tulchan.

When I asked him if had caught anything he replied, 'Yes – two salmon and a grilse.' I thought he said they were in the boat, but I could not see them and I even looked in the boot of the car, thinking I might have misheard him. He then told me that they were on two strings attached to the rowlocks, one on each side, and were still alive, the object being to keep them fresh. Two salmon were. tied to one string passed through the gills and the other string held the grilse in similar fashion.

I did not like it because I felt that it was tormenting the fish, and I told him so. I insisted on putting them out of their misery then, rather than at the end of the day. Reluctantly, he went to pull the fish in and at least I had the pleasure of seeing the grilse escape as he was doing so.

As usually happens, Bob had to enjoy his satisfaction in silence, as he did on another occasion when a party of anglers insisted on rowing themselves across the Ash Tree pool, at Kinnaird. The wide pool is turbulent at all heights with whirling water in the middle but, assured that the man doing the rowing was an Atlantic yachtsman, he agreed to let them try. The boat ended up two pools lower down!

Professional as they are, ghillies sometimes blunder, and many of us have lost good fish as a result. The only thing to do is sympathise, but sometimes it is difficult. Don Macer-Wright recalls an error of judgement which rather embarrassed him at the time.

When I was looking after the Littlecote water on the Kennet, in the midsummer of 1972, I noticed a large fish basking under a big willow on the other side and assumed that it was a pike, which we did not want in the water. I went over to the other bank but could not see it there at all, so I decided to try for it from the far side. All I had with me was a 7-foot brook rod with which I managed to cast a tiny fly spoon to within sight of the fish. At the second cast the fish took, hooked itself and headed downstream. I then saw that it was, in fact, a monster brown trout which, of course, it was the prerogative of the members to catch.

I walked him down and into the net before he realised what was happening. A lovely cock fish in fine condition, he weighed 9¼ pounds. I suppose that I should have put it back, but it was agreed by some members who were present that such a monster was better out of the river. There happened to be a Church fete in the Rectory garden, at Chilton Foliat, on the following day so it was decided to sell it there. Presumably it had begun to smell because of the heat but, whatever the reason, there was no buyer. Later, to my dismay, I discovered that the fish had been unceremoniously dumped on the Littlecote rubbish tip, which seemed a sad end to the biggest trout I had ever caught, if somewhat by accident. So I rescued it and cut off the head, which still serves me as a rather gruesome paperweight.

Tom Batho, who lives on the Test near Whitchurch, gave me an unusual example of somewhat unprofessional behaviour by a ghillie.

A very experienced water-keeper on the Test was asked to give two rich but inexperienced fishermen a demonstration of how to catch a fish. On looking into the water he saw a large pike and explained to his charges that it was legitimate to pull out a pike by means of a noose. He tied a rabbit snare to a stick and then edged it carefully over the pike's tail. Yanking hard, he threw himself backwards with all his force. Sadly, he had not appreciated that he was standing directly in front of a tree and knocked himself out. His pupils, who had the task of reviving him, were not impressed by his prowess.

Don Macer-Wright recalled a river-keeper who was rather more adept at removing the cannibals.

When I was the river keeper on the St Cross beat of the Itchen below Winchester, around 1967, the keeper of the College water above me had seen three large pike close together in one of his pools. He caught two of them, weighing 23 and 24 pounds, and shortly afterwards, when I was helping him to electro-fish the water, I caught the other which was just under 20. I think that 66 pounds of pike from one hole must be something of a record. I learned later than another of 30 pounds had been taken from the same place.

It is sad, perhaps, that on a lot of trout waters grayling are looked upon as almost as damaging as pike because they eat so much of the trout food, and are removed whenever possible. Don Macer-Wright discovered how to get the really big ones.

When I was keepering on the Itchen, it was renowned for its big grayling. A 2-pound grayling is an unusual fish but one afternoon I landed two, each weighing 4^{1}/$_{2}$ pounds, inside an hour. They would take nothing until I discovered the deadly method of a sinking bread pellet which had to be made from sliced, white bread. This gave off what looked like an oily slick, and perhaps that attracted the fish.

I was proud of my monster grayling, but soon afterwards I witnessed the capture of a 5^{1}/$_{2}$-pounder above the St Cross road bridge. Later still, a 7-pound grayling was taken on the Abbots Barton water while it was being electrically fished.

It is always fun to spring a surprise on a ghillie, so long as it is a pleasant one! I have recorded my penchant for hand-lining in logs which turn out to be salmon and Jim Tritton, the ghillie on Upper Kinnaird, told me of a not dissimilar event which happened there in September 1992.

Father and son Thompson come up from the south to fish with me, the junior being a great joker. He was spinning from the bank below my hut when he noticed that he was in trouble with his

Chapter 13

Ghillies' Stories

Stephen Jones, the river keeper on the Chilton beat of the Kennet, near where I live, began his active career at Broadlands where, from the example of Bernard Aldrich, he learned a great deal. As is common practice on many rivers, the stews where young fish were being reared were protected at night from poachers and vandals by trip wires which fired 12-bore cartridges when actuated. The lead pellets, of course, had been removed and the main object was to scare intruders and induce them to believe that one of the Broadlands keepers would hear the bang and come tearing down. For good measure, each empty cartridge case was filled with malachite crystals, which will stain bright green anything with which they come into contact. This could be evidence of the trespass with intent should the intruder be caught, but was mainly to cause him maximum inconvenience. Early one morning the device worked perfectly in trapping a couple of most unexpected intruders, as Stephen told me.

It was the habit of the late Earl Mountbatten, in the late 1970s, to put in some extra hours of riding round the Broadlands estate as practice for the Trooping of the Colour. Being very busy, he usually did this before breakfast. At 7 am one morning, before the bangers had been deactivated for the day, there was a loud report from the area of the stew-ponds and one of the staff, who was about half a mile a way, realised, with horror, what must have happened. He raced down to see Lord Mountbatten on a frisky horse which had a bright green backside. Fortunately, his lordship was highly amused as he galloped away, although I do not imagine that the groom who had to wash the dye off thought it so funny.

My dogs have occasionally discharged the bangers on the stretch of the Kennet where my husband and I fish but, happily, have never been stained – yet.

The older hands at Broadlands played tricks on the young apprentices, as Stephen recalled when we chatted by the Kennet.

There was a large cork tree at Broadlands, near where the lawns sweep down to the river, and I had not been there long when

112

multiplier reel. I happened to come by and took the rod from him
and untangled a bird's nest, which took a few minutes. When I
had finished he said, 'You know that I've got a salmon on the end
of this line.'

'Oh yes,' I replied, handing him back the rod.

He took it, tightened the line and a salmon leapt from the water.
I shook my head in sheer disbelief. I had never seen anyone so
unperturbed when he knew he was into a salmon, especially in
these days of scarcity.

I have met one woman gamekeeper, at Longwood in Hampshire, when
it was a major pheasant shoot. In fact, she was expert enough to write
a book about the profession. But until I was asked to fish the Wye at
Lydbrook in the spring of 1989 I had never heard of a woman ghillie.
There she was, larger than life and, at 20 years old, not only feminine
but extremely competent. Her name was Lynn Woodward and she was
then believed to be the only female ghillie in England. This suggests,
perhaps, that there was one or more in Scotland, but if so I have never
encountered one.

In the course of that pleasant day it was quickly apparent that Lynn
was capable of doing everything that was required. In her green,
broad-brimmed hat loaded with fishing badges, her knickerbockers,
waxed jacket and boots, she certainly looked the part. And it was no
illusion. First, she knew the long beat backwards and exactly where
fish were likely to lie and – just as importantly – where they did not lie.
She was also adept at working the rowing boats and motor boats from
which most of the fishing is done at most heights of water, and proved
to be a knowledgeable angler with the capacity, like many ghillies, for
catching salmon.

It was no surprise to me that my husband chose to spend the day with
this slim, auburn-haired girl and she it was, after a blank session with
the fly and spinner, who indoctrinated him into the considerable art of
worm fishing for salmon. She announced that she possessed 10 large
lobworms as he watched her mount three of them on a large hook.
She used a short line, and within minutes, a fish began plucking at the
line. She passed the rod to my husband, telling him when to strike.
The method produced a 10-pound fish with sea-lice, the only salmon
caught that day.

Lynn, who was also a good companion in the boat, turned out to
have two A Levels but chose to be a professional ghillie because she
loves the way of life. Her father was Lydbrook's head ghillie, and she
had been brought up on the river and could not face an inside job.
Her father did nothing either to encourage or to deter her, and the
partnership worked out well.

119

While ghillies usually get fair tips nobody would choose the job for the financial return, which is modest over the year. But Lynn not only enjoyed her work but also most of the many different people she has met. And when you are in a boat all day with people, you really do *meet* them. In the course of only a few hours you are likely to see them in many moods – hopeful, bored, excited and often dejected. The boasters – and angling has its share of them – quickly reveal their failings, as do the incompetent anglers.

There would seem to be only one professional disadvantage to being a woman ghillie – the physical problem of dealing with salmon poachers, who can be violent these days when cornered. Fortunately both Lynn and her father had a close link with the local police, and with their ever-ready walkie-talkies were in quick communication.

What does an attractive girl ghillie do with her spare time? At the end of a long day, when most of her charges were only too happy to have an early night, Lynn was at the local disco, dancing away with a boyfriend and enjoying a few drinks.

She may have to give up her aquatic career if she marries, but if so I am sure that it will be with a heavy heart.

Meanwhile, I trust that she will not be subjected to the same experience as Peter Woolnough, the keeper on the stretch of the Kennet where we fish. His was certainly a tale of the most unexpected.

My cottage is situated near the River Aldbourne which, before the days of serious water abstraction, used to carry good trout and was part of our fishing. I knew that I was being poached by two local yobbos who used a motor-bike, and I was anxious to catch them. One evening my wife told me that she had seen two men on a motor-cycle, with crash helmets, who had ridden up one of the private banks. So, after arming myself with an axe handle, I crept up there quietly. When I found them they were lying on a blanket and were both stark naked, and one of them was a woman. I do not know who among the three of us was the most embarrassed. I turned away, but they stayed only long enough to put their clothes on and roar away.

More in keeping with the eerie nature of most tales of the unexpected was the story told to me by Michael Kelton, from Churt in Surrey, over lunch. It is well known that Scottish ghillies tend to be superstitious but this experience goes beyond anything else I have heard.

I was fishing the Lower Torrish pool of the Helmsdale, which had long been the favourite of a friend of ours who had just died and had been regarded by the ghillie there as a brilliant angler. Anthony Nutting, who owned the beat, agreed that the angler's ashes should be scattered there, as he had wished, and this was duly done. Although it had been a good season and there were fish in the river, nothing was caught in that famous pool for the ensuing three weeks. This seemed peculiar to us, although the ghillie seemed to regard it as inevitable.

Then someone hooked a big salmon which took ages to land. It deployed every trick and exploited every rock as though it was remarkably familiar with the pool. When it was eventually landed, it weighed 22 pounds, and as the ghillie administered the last rites with the priest he said, seriously and with obvious satisfaction, 'We've got him at last! The fishing will be OK now.'

Oddly enough, it was.

Most women know that they should never allow their husbands to teach them how to drive. By the same token, they should also avoid getting their husbands to ghillie for them when salmon fishing, as so much can so easily go wrong? I was lucky in that my husband was on hand in time to extract my first salmon, a 13-pounder on the River Slaney in Ireland, but others have been less fortunate, as David Shaw has put on record.

When my wife and frequent trout-fishing companion, Kate, announced her determination to catch a salmon, it was certainly on the cards. After three years of catching trout successfully it was obviously going to be just a matter of time before the day came – as it did. When a tremendous downpour topped up the rough little Highland river by which we were staying, drenching me to the skin at the same time, I was forced to make an unscheduled return to the cottage, where Kate was busy in the kitchen. Looking out of the window and down into the valley, she noticed that the weather was giving way to clear blue sky, as can happen so dramatically in those parts, and decided that the time had come. 'Think that stretch is worth a try?' she asked, referring to where the river, in full flood, tumbled away round a forested corner.

I felt that it would be better to let the water fine down a bit but could see no harm in her having a go. So off we went, Kate with the grilse rod, me with my trout rod. We stopped where I thought I might have a chance with a brownie under some bank alders using a wet fly. Kate decided to have a try in the Corner pool, 200 yards or so below, so I removed my big collapsible salmon net, showed her how to strap it on to her back and how to release and extend it. Finally, with everything adjusted, Kate asked. 'If I do get something on you'll come down and help me, won't you?' I assured her that she need only shout and I would be there.

From time to time I ventured a glance downstream where

I could see Kate working patiently away, although sometimes
obscured by a bush. I do not suppose that more than half an hour
had passed when, glancing downstream, I was confronted by an
alarming sight. By the violence of Kate's gestures I realised that
something was amiss and, although I could hear nothing, I wasted
no time in getting beside her. Her face was flushed and her eyes
as wide as saucers. 'I lost him! I lost that – fish! Where were you?
Fine – ghillie you are! I screamed till I was hoarse.'

I assured her that I had heard nothing above the roar of the
stream and that she must have been behind a bush. Kate sat on a
rock, shaking and clearly in a state of 'lost-fish' shock.

'I had him on for at least 10 minutes,' she moaned. 'I had
him right on to the shingle. I got the net unstrapped and partly
extended but I couldn't get him into it.'

She was not to be easily consoled. She had hooked her fish,
which appeared to have been in the 12–15-pound class, on a tiny
Black Pennell, and how she had managed to hold it in the little
pool I shall never know. Yet it was not until she had had it on the
shingle that it had managed the quick flip that dislodged the hook.

That evening, when she had settled down and I told her she had
done wonderfully well to hold on to it, she looked at me and said
'If you were really my ghillie, by now you'd have been fired.'

Two summers later, with Kate still blank for salmon, David com-
pounded the felony, although in a different way.

Having promised Kate that, as a consolation prize, she alone
would fish the Corner pool in future and that her ghillie would
always remain in close attendance while she did so, we were
back there together. Again the water was on the high side and
it was about the same time of day – the afternoon. I made sure
that the joints of her double-handed rod were secure, that the
cast and the knots were sound. I watched her from a little way
upstream, where there was no possibility that I could repeat my
last performance. She fished the pool most ably but gave up when
she was convinced that nothing was moving or was likely to. I
suggested that she should give it another run through, offering
to go without dinner, but she was determined to return to the
kitchen. 'Mind leaving the rod with me?' I asked. She gave it to
me, wishing me luck.

I fished through her pool. She had been right. There was no
sign of life. But before packing in for the day, I decided on a few
casts into the fast water running down into the pool below. My
Black Shrimp single was just coming round on my second cast
when a sizeable brown back turned gently in the broken water,

'Damn this net'

20 yards downstream, and I was into a fine, strong fish. It was not easy to play the spirited little salmon in the confined stretch of water, but after 15 minutes of clambering over rocks and a barbed-wire fence I managed to extract him. Wending my way back to the cottage the problem was how to break the news.

'Any luck?' Kate asked.

'Come and look,' I replied quietly, and out she came to see a clean, 7-pound salmon lying on the grass.

When I assured her that I had not caught it in her pool but in the run below she countered, 'I see. You were saving that bit until I left.'

Chapter 14

Unlucky Fish

While every angler has a share of bad luck, fish – and salmon in particular – experience it more often and, of course, with rather more serious consequences, as Bruce Penney described to me while I was resting from fishing on the Little Blackhall beat of the Dee.

On the Hampshire Avon, at Ibsley village, there are two arches to the bridge. Fishing there, on the right bank, I heard a salmon splash by the near arch, waded out and put an upstream worm to it. The salmon eventually took, ran upstream through the near arch and promptly came down through the far one. There was nothing to do but let all the line go, tearing it off the reel in the hope that the fish would stop when it felt no pressure, which it did.

My companion that day was fishing on the other bank with a bait and he was able to hook my line and he pulled it in until he could grasp it. He then cut it and knotted it to his own line, having removed his bait. The fish was still on and he began to play it so that it looked as though he was going to land a fish which I had hooked. The salmon had other ideas, however. It went back upstream though the arch down which it had come and then proceeded to go downstream through the arch on my side to the lie where it had been originally. I therefore repeated the process, using a Toby to catch the line, cutting it and tying it to my own. That way I eventually killed the fish I had hooked myself – a 17-pounder.

Bruce seems to specialise in such capers, as he went on to relate as I sat on the bank, fascinated, with my tape-recorder at the ready.

Fishing with a fly, I hooked a salmon which became snagged round a rock. My friend, who was on the other side of the river fishing a Toby, hooked my line to try and free it. In the process, the Toby slid down the line and hooked the salmon in the jaw, so for a short time we were both into the fish. In the ensuing struggle, however, the fly came out and the fish was successfully

125

One way to catch a salmon

played and landed by the spinner. The salmon had taken a fly but was landed on a bait!

My surgeon friend, Tony Richards, from the Hampshire Clinic, succeeded with rather more 'cowboy' methods.

A few years ago I was fishing the Junction pool of the Upper Beaulieu, in the first week of July. The beats below the dam had caught a lot of salmon, but by Friday we had not been able to hook a single fish. I was using a 10-pound cast, but had unwisely economised by using some old, lightweight nylon for the dropper, which carried a small fly. At the tail of the pool I had my first offer and managed to land a nice salmon of 12 pounds. A few casts later, from the same lie, I landed another, smaller salmon. I started again in the neck of the pool and hooked another fish on the dicey dropper. Sure enough, it broke as I was trying to beach it, but within a second the reel was singing again and I realised that I must have foul-hooked the fish. I assumed that the point fly had hooked it but when I eventually beached the fish, tail first – about 600 yards downstream – I found that it was lassoed right round the tail, just as it would have been had I used a tailer. The fish was fresh and weighed 10^1/2 pounds. The tail fly had been well named!

David Browse of Liss, Hampshire, sent me a variant on the lucky angler-unlucky fish theme.

On the River Itchen, where I fish, before the hatches were rebuilt and a salmon pass was installed, there was a splendid lie close under the right bank, a few yards upstream of the hatch, where a fish, having struggled through, would often stop for a breather. Standing on top of the hatch one July morning, and looking upstream, I spotted a tail. So, having tackled up well away from the stream, I drifted a natural brown Shrimp down towards the fish. Immediately there was a flash, accompanied by a savage take. The salmon spent most of the next five minutes in the air and, when in the water, was moving at great speed all over the river.

As suddenly as it had started, the activity stopped, the fish just trod water in mid-stream above the centre hatch. It stayed there until I tried to walk it upstream, when it followed me, as all the text-books tell one it should, but only for some 6 or 7 yards. Then off it went again, but this time back through the hatch into the pool below, leaving me with something of a problem.

Having hit on a possible solution, I let the salmon take all the line it wanted, hoping that the hook would hold, and left the rod propped up with the clutch of the reel set to allow more line to run if the fish pulled any more. Fortunately, I had already tackled

up a small spinning rod with a Number 4 Mepp spoon attached
and going down on to the bank of the pool I managed to hook the
line with the Mepp and carefully brought it to the bank without
disturbing the fish. I then pulled off more line from the rod above
the hatch, cut it and tied it to the spinning line, having taken off
the Mepp. The fish was still on and, after a further brief fight, I
was able to net a sea-liced salmon of 9^1/$_2$ pounds. Very exciting!

There are very few experienced salmon fishers who have not inadvertently foul-hooked a salmon and having landed it, usually after a long
run downstream, wondered whether the sporting thing to do would
be to put it back. The current view is that such a prolonged struggle
is likely to prove fatal to the fish anyway, because of a lethal build-up
of muscle waste products in the system, but a few purists still return
them, as Michael Parry, a shooting friend, and a very distinguished
lady both saw.

> The Queen Mother was fishing the Dee near Balmoral, where
> the river is quite narrow. A man on the other side foul-hooked
> a salmon, played it and, feeling that the presence of the Queen
> Mother required him to do the sporting thing, returned it to the
> water after beaching it.
> Sound carries easily across water and the Queen Mother was
> heard to observe to her ghillie: 'Bloody fool! Putting a fresh
> fish back.'

I have already recorded one extraordinary story of a fouled line in
the vastness of the sea. My neighbour, Michael Stevenson, told me
of another.

> In July 1991, I went with four friends to Alaska where, after
> five good days of salmon fishing, we heard about some fantastic
> halibut fishing off a place called Homer. Two of us decided that
> we would give it a try.
> We had heard that there was a monthly competition for the
> largest halibut, with prizes like $20,000. As the largest fish to date
> that month had been 117 pounds we thought we might be in with
> a chance, so we bought some $5 tickets and set off at 6 am for
> the fishing grounds where, of course, other boats were already
> hard at it.
> My friend hooked into a fish and was astonished when he could
> not reel it in. When the boatman confirmed that it was indeed a
> fish the deck was cleared in anticipation of a monster. Though the
> lucky angler weighed 15 stones he still could not heave the fish to
> the surface after 15 minutes, saying that it was like to trying to lift
> a garage door off the bottom. The prospect of $20,000, however,

kept him going. By the time he was exhausted, a 20-pound halibut
appeared, to cries of 'If that's what a little halibut can do . . .'
Further inspection, however, showed that there was another
line attached with 6 pounds of lead weight and a long length of
someone else's line, which had broken. Clearly two fishermen has
been playing each other both thinking they were into a winner.

We caught about 80 halibut in the day, all under 100 pounds,
but another boat hauled in one of 277 pounds, which did win that
month's competition.

Chapter 15

Eccentrics

I suppose that to non-fishers all dedicated anglers seem rather eccentric, especially those who spend many hours staring at a float. While I must, of course, profoundly disagree, I sometimes wonder about the coarse fishers whom I see on the Kennet-Avon canal at the back of our house. What I have in mind is the amount of tackle that they carry with them – so much these days that many of them are driven to using trolleys. They may have as many as six rods, even more reels and a chest of drawers containing enough ancillary tackle to start a shop, as well as several trays of maggots of different sizes and colours. (I have heard it said that some maggot fishers keep the hook baits in their mouths to liven them up!) They must all be thankful that, as they never kill a fish – it is almost a crime to do so – they do not also have to carry their catch at the end of the day, as trout and salmon anglers have to. I have sometimes had to lug a salmon back half a mile up the banks of the Dee to the hut and, in chest waders, with all the tackle as well, it is quite an effort. I suppose that, when seen by someone strolling along the opposite bank, I look eccentric too. I would certainly have done so to any non-fishing motorist passing through the main street of Grantown-on-Spey on a hot July day a few years ago.

Having decided to change after we got back to the lodge on our last day, a Saturday, I thought I would buy a few things in the local shops. As I walked from one shop to another in my chest waders, and still wearing my floppy hat, my husband said that all I needed was a diver's helmet. Yet in that town well used to salmon fishers, nobody even noticed. If we anglers are all eccentric, then there is safety in numbers. There are more than four million of us but, as I say, everything depends on circumstances, as witness the extraordinary story told to me by Roy Bush.

As I was fishing in a match on Sunday I was early to bed on Saturday, setting the alarm for a pre-dawn call that would give me plenty of time to get ready and catch the coach. The alarm did not let me down and, as it was winter, I put on plenty of warm clothes. The last thing I do is put on my watch and, as I did so that morning, I realised that I had set the alarm nearly two hours too early. I therefore decided to go back to bed for an hour

130

All the gear

without undressing. I crept between the sheets quietly so as not to disturb my wife, but she was half-awake and I explained what had happened as I snuggled down. She moved over to me, cuddling up, but was suddenly wide awake, saying, 'Roy, your legs are freezing!'

'That's not my legs,' I replied. 'I've still got my waders on.' Her comments are unprintable.

One ardent angler who admits to eccentricity in a way unusual in itself is Colin Farnell who fishes the same water that I do.

I believe that few people can have loved fly fishing for trout more than I have and, until about eight years ago, I would have said that nothing could have diverted my attention from the sport once I was down on the Littlecote stretch of the River Kennet, where I have fished for the last 20 years. That, however, was before I became smitten by an urge which some might, with justification, call arborimania.

The four Littlecote beats, with a total length of some 3¹/2 miles, are outstandingly beautiful and peaceful, but there were parts which I could see could be improved, both from the aesthetic and the angling points of view. They were bare of trees, which would not only enhance the surroundings but provide a windbreak and encourage insect life, of which all rivers have become increasingly deprived. There was one particular stretch, on the Home beat near the great house, which was difficult to fish when the wind was anywhere near the north, so I sought the owner's permission to plant a few trees there on the side of the river opposite to that where we stand to fish. It was gladly given and I set to work without delay. Little did I know what I was starting.

Clearly, the trees on the Home beat had to be specimens and I contented myself with eight which, after taking advice from various nurseries, I planted myself. If I could have afforded big trees, which are now available but at a high cost, I could have seen a quick result but, as I had to plant them, they had to be small anyway. It took time which, of course, had to come out of my fishing hours on the river because I have to earn my living so there is a limit to the time I can spend there in any one week. What I had not fully appreciated when I began was the regular maintenance necessary to keep young trees from being overgrown by weeds. I had to do that too, with a little grass hook, and that ate up more fishing time.

Nevertheless, I was so hooked on the idea of embellishing the river that I soon spotted other parts which were sorely in need of trees, and I was driven to provide them. In some areas I ended up planting what amounted to little spinneys. To date, I have procured and planted more than 600 trees, mainly deciduous, such as copper beech, copper hazel, willows of seven kinds, silver birch, limes, wild cherry and alders, but a few of them conifers, like larch and swamp cyprus. In addition, my urge to beautify the scene induced me to plant scores of flowering shrubs – buddleia, forsythia, hibiscus, philadelphus, kerria and smoke bush. My problem is that I am a perfectionist and cannot bear a job which is not properly or fully done.

In the process, I learned a great deal, such as the folly of planting tiny trees which have no hope of survival. I learned how much maintenance is involved and the time and effort it takes, although the estate foresters now help me in a major clear-out of undergrowth each June, which takes a team of two professionals two and a half days.

I was aware that my angling colleagues had begun to doubt my sanity as they saw me toiling away while the trout were rising, for there were days when I never had time to put my rod up at all. Their suspicions were strengthened by the fact that I was planting these expensive permanent fixtures on somebody else's land. Farnell's trees became something of a joke and have even been the subject of a few curses when fishermen have caught their flies in them.

Although I have now planted enough I know that I will never finish because, apart from the maintenance, there are always a few casualities and I have committed myself to replacing them. It has all cost me more than I care to think, but I have no regrets. When I see my trees and plants again at the beginning of each season they are a little nearer to maturity and I sense that others are beginning to appreciate their beauty and their value. I have written my signature on the river-banks which have given me so much enjoyment in a way which should long outlast me when 'in the Lord's safe landing net I am peacefully asleep'.

As for the arborimania, well, it is just another incurable disease on top of the one from which all my fellow anglers also suffer – fishing.

Normally those who let trout fishing by the day are solicitous of their customers because they need them to come again, but Michael Stevenson, a Hungerford fish farmer who supplies trout fisheries, encountered one set in a different mould.

While I was stocking a lake in Oxfordshire with rainbow trout, the owner spotted one of his fisherman walking towards us. 'Oh God! It's that wretched man!' he said. 'I wish I could get rid of him.'

He then explained that the angler was forever complaining – either there were no fish or they were too small, although all his other customers seemed satisifed.

When the fisherman reached us he looked in the bin of trout we were about to unload into the lake and saw a fish of 2 pounds on the top. 'That's the sort of fish I want to catch,' he cried. 'I don't want to see any fish smaller than that.'

My client asked to borrow the angler's landing net, dipped the two largest trout out of the bin and slapped them into his hands. 'There, and that's your limit so you can go home!'

Open-mouthed, the angler walked away speechless. I doubt whether he ever returned.

Ghillies lead such an unusual life that it would be surprising if some of them were not eccentric. My old friend Ian Anderson, of the Upper Blackhall beat on the Dee, was certainly offbeat in carrying a shooting stick and an umbrella, although it made good sense to remain dry. I would not class Bob Grant of the Tay as eccentric, but one remark he made to me suggested an unusual attitude, to say the least. At the end of a flat and unrewarding day I told him that I had been calculating the number of casts I had made and it turned out to be about 400. 'Ah well,' he said, 'that's another 400 casts you don't have to make'.

I suppose that's one way of looking at salmon fishing these days.

Chapter 16

Fishing Dogs

Most of the fishing stories about dogs which have come my way concern Labradors and I suspect that there are two reasons for this. First, many anglers also shoot and the Labrador, being the commonest shooting dog today, is therefore the likeliest companion dog on the river. Secondly, Labradors have the fishing instinct rooted in their genes because they were originally developed to retrieve fish. The breed was established by the sea fishermen of Newfoundland, who fished mainly for cod from small boats using long lines baited with hundreds of hooks. Many of the cod fell off the hooks when the lines were being drawn in and their dogs would leap into the sea and retrieve them – their thick, double coats enabling them to withstand the wintry water.

As there were no refrigeration ships in the early part of the last century the fishermen could export their fish only by drying and salting it, and Poole, in Dorset, was one of the British ports to which they brought it. A certain Earl of Malmesbury heard about the remarkable ability of Labradors to retrieve from water because, when the ships were berthed at Poole, the fishermen would sometimes entertain the locals by throwing objects into the dock and the dogs would recover them. The Earl, an avid wildfowler, assumed that they could be trained to recover ducks, so he acquired a breeding stock. And that, basically, is the origin of the breed which now dominates the shooting field.

Anyone watching our chocolate Labrador, Dido, (who is now famous in her own right as an author, having produced two books) would readily accept that there is something 'fishy' in her nature because, without training, she is absolutely fascinated by every aspect of angling, whether it be for salmon, trout or even coarse fish. She is a welcome friend to the anglers on the Kennet-Avon canal behind our house.

When my husband and I are fishing she sits where she can see the fly and immediately, becomes excited when either of us hooks a trout, appearing to know exactly where to position herself so that she can be in at the kill when we net it. She can sense the difference between the noise of the reel when a fish is pulling line off and when I am, and ignores the latter. She is keen to try to retrieve the fish, but that would cause too much disturbance for the other members of our club.

135

One day, however, when there is nobody else about, I am sure that I will be tempted. Since Dido published her first book, *One Dog and Her Man*, several anglers have written to say that they allow their Labradors to land all their trout, enabling them to dispense with landing nets. This would suit me, especially as it is the one item of tackle I tend to leave behind.

Dido never barks when we hook a trout, but always does so when we hook a salmon. As my husband and I are usually at least one pool apart, and he allows me the service of the ghillie, this behaviour has more than once served the purpose of letting the ghillie know that my husband was into a fish and sent him racing down to assist.

As I have related earlier, Dido was once pegged down on the bank when I could have drowned in the Tay, so we now leave her free. Being such a strong dog she might make all the difference if an accident befalls either of us in the future, although we are now equipped with flotation jackets.

A Flat-coat Retriever which belonged to Colin Farnell before its regrettable demise, and which I often saw on the Kennet, would sit quietly while he was fishing but as soon it saw him hook a trout, and without being told, it would go to find the fish-bass which was lying on the bank and bring it so that it was handy. However, I have to award the fisherdog's palm to a liver and white Springer Spaniel belonging to my dear friend, Massimo Coen, a Venetian domiciled in London for many years. Here is his story as he told it.

It was a cold January morning in the Welney Washes and the shooting season would be ending within a few days. So why not take a rod as well and try for a pike?

With two companions I walked down the wash in the darkness, placed the baited rod on the bank of the River Delph and returned to our hides, hoping for a duck or two. The dawn came, we had a few shots and then came the moment when one is sure that it is pointless to wait any longer. So back we went to spend some time with the rod. To our dismay it had disappeared, but we soon saw the big float bobbing up and down in the middle of the river. As we were wondering what to do, I noticed Rocket, my splendid Springer, looking at me enquiringly. That was it! 'Fetch it,' I cried and Rocket leapt in and swam towards the float. He grabbed it but was soon in trouble, for as fast as he pulled towards the bank he was pulled the other way. Clearly, he was playing a sizeable fish. All we could do was to cheer him on and our excitement was intense as he desperately tried to land himself and beach the pike. Eventually he succeeded in reaching dry land and the tussle continued. We decided not to assist, except by cheering

136

even more loudly, and he backed up the bank with a great deal
of flapping in the shallow water. A few moments later he had a
9-pound pike high and dry, having played and landed it unaided.
I have never been so excited watching a companion play a fish.
Rocket was rewarded with my last chicken sandwich and we duly
blooded him.

My intrepid fisherdog died at the age of 14, much mourned and
never to be forgotten.

Some gundogs, however, can be less than helpful, even obstreperous,
on a river, as Jim Tritton, the ghillie on the Upper Kinnaird beat of
the Tay, remembered.

Kenny White, who lives at Falkirk, is a worm fisher and has an
occasional day with me. A great joker, he was playing a salmon by
the hut unbeknown to me, when I was fishing in the boat further
down. I had left my young black Labrador, Spey, in my garden
but he got out, ran down to Kenny and, for some reason, started
rogering his leg while he was playing the fish. He tried hard to get
rid of him but the dog was determined to hang on.

Eventually Kenny landed the salmon with Spey still firmly
grasping. It had been unintentional but I reckon that it compensated
for a few of Kenny's old scores. I was only sorry that I had not
been there with my camera.

Tony Samuel who for many years was the fortunate owner of the
magnificent Arndilly beat of the Spey, kindly supplied me with the
following canine contribution.

One morning I was fishing the Soo pool at Arndilly and had
dispatched my wife, Mercy, who was fairly new to salmon
fishing, to Coble Pot, the pool immediately above. She was in
sight of me and the ghillie, John Macdonald, who was assisting me
because Soo is a difficult place to land a fish and is also renowned
for hazardous wading. While I was playing a largeish salmon
I looked upstream and saw that Mercy was also playing a fish.
Being the usual husband, and knowing that there was a small
sandy place where she could beach her fish, I told the ghillie to
stay with me until we had landed ours. This achieved, I looked up
to see Mercy standing on the edge of the sandy beach waving her
arms and obviously in some distress. I told Macdonald to race up
to her, having knocked my fish on the head, and I walked after
him, slowly, as was my wont.

It transpired that while Mercy had been playing her fish her
rod had broken at the butt. With great presence of mind, she had
proceeded to play the fish off her hands, recovering the line and

Rocket the spaniel lands a pike

paying it out as though from a ball of wool. Luckily, she was wearing gloves, which saved her from friction burns. Finally she had beached the salmon with great skill but, disliking the idea of picking up the fish, she had held it between her feet with her back to the water until help should arrive. Unfortunately, her Labrador had run up in the excitement and had broken the line, but she had managed to contain the fish until Macdonald reached her. 'Oh Mrs Samuel,' he observed, 'you should have a priest!', to which, being new to the sport, she replied, 'What the hell could he have done to help me?'

Dido has not yet caused any trouble while I have been playing a fish but she ruined one evening's trout fishing, causing us dismay for a couple of days and setting up a fishy record likely to stand for all time. One July evening, my husband, Harry, was standing on a bank casting into a deep pool and hooked a trout which jumped and threw the fly out of its mouth. The fly flew back towards him and, Dido, who was sitting close by, snapped at it, perhaps thinking it was one of these horrible horse flies which had been annoying all three of us. Harry put down his rod and opened Dido's mouth. He was horrified to find that the fly had disappeared and seemed to be in her throat with the nylon cast wrapped round her teeth. He cut the nylon, leaving about 18 inches on the fly, and called me out of the hut close by, where I was having a drink with a guest.

Dido was spluttering as she tried to spit out the offensive object, eating bits of grass to aid the process by making her sick, but without success. By that time, Harry had decided on a rush visit to the vet, who might be hard to find at that time. It looked like being a case for surgery in a nasty place, with almost certainly need for a general anaesthetic. In some agitation, he took her to the car, but by the time they got there the dog had ceased to be distressed and there was nothing to be seen in her mouth. So, having decided that there was no longer any point in taking her to the vet he brought her back to the river where Peter, the keeper, agreed that she seemed to be quite normal and must have spat the fly out, although we could see no signs of it.

Nevertheless, we remained greatly concerned by the possibility that the sharp, barbed hook of the fly might be sticking somewhere in Dido's gut and cause an abscess or even a haemorrhage. 'The acid in a dog's stomach is very strong,' Harry told me reassuringly. 'I suppose that it might be strong enough to dissolve the steel of the hook.' It is astonishing what straws the human mind will grasp to console itself. The length of nylon posed its own danger, because it can ensnare a section of the intestine.

Dido seemed fine when we put her to bed on her bean bag but I crept down during the small hours to reassure myself, and so did Harry. All seemed well next morning when Harry, who usually brings me breakfast in bed while I read the newspapers, decided that, for his peace of mind at least, he should carry out what is known in hospitals as a stool examination. Dido has a dog door opening into a walled garden so there is usually an early-morning offering on the lawn. As a former zoologist he had no problem in dissecting each item with a couple of short, sharp sticks. Fortunately, he was out of sight of the neighbours, who might otherwise have doubted his sanity.

The investigation proved negative, and the following morning's researches looked like being the same until the great dissector reached the last specimen. Within it he discovered a little, flat packet of half-chewed grass, about the size of a postage stamp, and looking as though it had been carefully folded by a skilful hand. Within that he found the fly with the coil of nylon thread wrapped round it. The hook was as sharp and uncorroded as a new one.

With a cry of delight he washed it with a watering-can and carried it upstairs to show me the good news. Dangling the fly in front of my nose he announced 'To celebrate, I'm going to catch a fish with it!'

That evening we went down to the river. A few fish were rising and within minutes, in the pool where Dido's potentially dangerous accident had occurred, he had a 3-pound trout on the fly which had caused it. I doubt whether any other angler in history has ever caught a fish on a fly which has passed through a dog. It must be a record!

Inevitably, this episode gave Harry the idea of tying a fly with hairs from Dido's tail. So he cut some out and sent them off to a fly-tier to make a chocolate variant of a Stoat's Tail. He calls this fly a Dido and has since caught a salmon on it on the Little Blackhall beat of the Dee. It gave him great joy to say,' I caught it on a Dido.' However, the lady herself is worried that there might be a demand for Didos, as she is very proud of her otter's tail. Still, as I tell her, there is always a price to pay for immortality.

Chapter 17

Political Aspects

Somehow, one does not imagine the late Lord Beaverbrook, the self-made millionnaire and politician, as a fisherman, but as he told my husband, who knew him well, fishing was involved in a turning point in his life. He enjoyed fishing when he was a youth in Canada and one day, when he was alone in a boat on a trout lake among the real beavers, there was little doing. Suddenly he said to himself 'What the hell am I doing here? To hell with it!' He promptly packed up and left home to make his fortune. He was a millionaire at 30!

Lord Home of the Hirsel has been a lifelong fisherman with his own stretch on the Tweed. He kindly supplied me with an interesting story for *Fish Tales*. He could not assist me for this one but the late Sir Michael Hadow, a former Ambassador to Israel who lived nearby in Berkshire, provided one on his behalf.

In 1966, the Foreign Secretary, Sir Alec Douglas Home as he then was, made an official visit to Israel and asked me, as Ambassador, to set aside three days for a 'nature tour'. Knowing that he was a very keen fisherman, I included a trip to a kibbutz in the very north of Israel because the River Dan there had been stocked with trout. Sir Alec was fascinated by the idea and, though he did not say so, I imagine that he hoped he might be able to cast a fly with tackle provided there.

Sadly, all he saw was a 100-yard stretch of the river before it rounded a bend because beyond the bend Syrian snipers were installed in trenches about 400 yards away on the other side of the river, and they were in the habit of shooting at anyone fishing from the Israeli side.

General Abram Yoffee, who had retired from the army, was present and, while it might have occurred to him that having the British Foreign Secretary shot at by the Syrians could be in Israel's political interest, he forbade any closer inspection of the river.

Now that the Israelis control the far bank fishing is safe and there is even a trout farm there.

I never imagined that the late Lord Attlee would have any interest in fishing but according to Richard Haston of Coombe Bissett, Salisbury, who had access to the Test at Broadlands, he did.

At Lady Pamela Mountbatten's wedding to David Hicks in 1960 the former Prime Minister, Clement Attlee, was sitting in the pew in front of me. As the bride came up the aisle, Attlee leaned back and enquired 'How's the fishing?'

I also recall an occasion when Lord Mountbatten, then Chief of the Defence Staff, held a meeting of Service Chiefs at Broadlands. During a break they wandered down to the river and Mountbatten said to Air Chief Marshal Pike, 'With a name like yours you can't be allowed to leave without a fish.' I was asked to oblige and Pike was duly presented with the trout I had landed.

Fishing is never far from an angler's thoughts, as I realised when we attended the wedding of the daughter of a couple very dear to us, who own a most beautiful estate in Surrey, not far from Guildford. On a lovely day they were married outside a tiny chapel by a lake stocked with brown and rainbow trout. Wooden seats had been set up for the many guests, who included some distinguished politicians, in a setting which could hardly have been more romantic. When the trout began to rise in the middle of the ceremony, however I could see that my husband's interest was riveted on them, with the odd whispered utterance of 'Oh, that was a beauty!' I was only surprised that when the ceremony was over he attended the reception – I expected him to borrow a rod from the bride's father!

It may be stretching things to regard the story told me by John Sautelle Senior, a doyen of Australian angling, as 'political' but it was, in a way.

After the end of the Second World War, a friend and I used to pack-horse into the bush in search of fishing. The horses were supplied by a character who gave them peculiar names. One of them was called Petrov after the Russian KGB agent and so-called diplomat who had defected in Canberra in 1954, causing an international sensation.

'Why do you call him Petrov?' I asked the owner.

'Because he's a rushin' bastard,' he replied.

He certainly lived up to his name. As we approached the Indi river he backed and bolted, scattering the contents of his pack-saddle over about a mile of bush!

Stray thoughts at a wedding party

Chapter 18

Smoked Fish

Contrary to stories that stocked trout taste of either mud or nothing, the large brown trout and rainbows which we catch on the Kennet are delicious, especially when smoked. During the trout season my husband and I usually catch more than 20 rainbows, each weighing more than 5 pounds, which cold-smoke beautifully. I frequently serve smoked trout to guests, with no explanation, and I am often complimented on the delicacy of flavour of the 'smoked salmon'. Of course, there is no mistaking smoked salmon which has been made from a spring fish fresh from feeding in the sea, but the salmon which most fishermen send to the smoker are big ones which have been in the river for many weeks and are past their prime.

It is in connection with really prime smoked salmon that I have special reason to remember a German girl called Jutta, who was one of a succession of *au pair* girls of various nationalities who helped us out when we had a rather large country establishment. On one occasion, when we were away for a few days, we had left the fridge well stocked with food for Jutta, who had a large appetite, and I had forgotten that it also contained almost a whole side of smoked salmon. We were greeted on our return by Jutta's beaming comment 'Zmoked zalmon is zuper!' She had never experienced it before and had worked her way through the lot.

I told that story while lunching one day with our fishing friend and neighbour, Lord Sieff, the Life President of Marks and Spencer, and he capped it, as he so often does, with a better one.

It has long been my professional habit to wander around various Marks and Spencer stores to see things for myself at counter level. While doing this round the large branch at Marble Arch, a few years ago, I spotted my old friend Kirk Douglas, the film star, buying six sides of smoked salmon. 'What are going to do with them all?' I asked. 'Put on a huge party?' Kirk explained that he was taking them all back to the USA where he would deep-freeze them. I immediately ridiculed the idea, insisting that smoked salmon could not be deep-frozen successfully, which was the official view of our food experts, who had assured me that that our policy should be to discourage customers from attempting it.

Kirk simply said that the advice was rubbish because he had deep-frozen smoked salmon many times and, provided it was not left frozen for too long, it retained its texture and its taste. For my part, such was my trust in our experts that I still believed their advice to be correct.

Months later, when I was in America, I went to supper with Kirk Douglas and his wife. Smoked salmon was served and I commented most favourably on its quality. Kirk then told me that what we were eating was the last side of the six I had seen him buy, and which he had deep-frozen. I had to admit that I had been wrong and, on my return, the Marks and Spencer policy was changed. New tests were organised and showed, beyond question, that the smoked salmon can be satisfactorily deep-frozen so long as it is not left over-long.

A perennial problem is finding a really good fish smokery that is not too far away, especially when one is regularly catching large trout. All too often we have discovered a good one which supplies an excellent product, beautifully sliced and packed at reasonable price, only to find that it has closed down. Currently, our favourite smokery is run by the Test river keeper Jeff Hounslow, who encounters some interesting situations. Recently, he was able to resolve a mystery which had baffled several of his angling customers, who could not explain why a newcomer to their beat, who was a complete beginner, invariably caught his limit of two and a half brace, irrespective of weather and water conditions. Those who watched him from a distance noticed that he was in the habit of putting his left hand in his pocket at regular intervals, but could not fathom why.

One evening the angler arrived at Jeff's with his daily limit of five big rainbows to be smoked. When asked which fly he had been using he named several well-known patterns. The angler was accompanied by his guest, who asked Jeff if he would be kind enough to show him the best way of gutting a fish. Jeff seized one of the big rainbows and as he inserted the knife a handful of tinned sweetcorn suddenly appeared from its mouth.

'Ah,' said Jeff, 'I see you were also using a Jolly Green Corn fly.'

For that customer, who has not since reappeared, that incident was certainly a case of a tail and the unexpected!

Equally unexpected was the experience of an attractive young lady called Sue, who answered Jeff's advertisement for an assistant. At interview he asked her how she felt about filleting and slicing freshwater eels. She said she would have no qualms, but did not realise that they were alive, and that she would have to kill them. She picked up the bin containing the eels so gingerly that she knocked it over, while Jeff stood by helpless with laughter as she tried to pick up the wriggling eels from the floor. Sue not only got the job but is now Jeff's partner in the business at Chilbolton.

Jeff's saddest story concerns the most expert fisherman he had ever encountered. One day, when this man arrived by the river, he announced that, as the fishing was becoming too easy, he was going to cast only with his left hand to give the trout a more sporting chance. He did so, but still caught his quota.

Three days later the man's right hand was severed in a car accident. Once he had recovered, he hired the services of a professional one-armed angler and spent a day with him on the river to learn the tricks he had taught himself, such as tying on the fly with the aid of his teeth and holding the rod while manipulating the net.

The story says something about the unpredictability of Fate but more about the durability of the human spirit.

Chapter 19

Swords and the Unexpected

The media seem to relish any situation where a sportsman's quarry exacts some degree of revenge, even when it inflicts injury, as happened not long ago, when the twitching claw of a hen pheasant laid on the grass pressed the trigger of a shotgun which, incredibly, had been put down alongside, loaded and unsafe, beside it. My husband's nose bears witness to its unfortunate impact with a grouse he had shot, and I know of instances where people have been felled by falling pheasants. Anglers are sometimes wounded by their own hooks or gaffs while dealing with a salmon, but serious injuries actually inflicted by a fish are rare. However, I have secured first-hand accounts of two extraordinary occasions in which the quarry took savage revenge in what so many people regard as a safe and peaceful sport. The first is told by the victim, Robert Breden of Chelsea, Victoria, Australia, who was already a champion big-game fisherman with many trophies when the encounter occurred.

On 22 January 1991, four days after my seventeenth birthday, I went fishing with four friends off Montagu Island in a 21-foot Donzi boat. Having overslept, we did not leave Bermagui until about 11 am and had travelled about 20 miles along the coast towards Narooma, fishing mainly for yellowtail kingfish with mackerel out on a 10-kilogram (22-pound) breaking strain line.

Eventually the line took off and 12-year-old Nicola Hill grabbed the rod. There was such a swirl that we all thought it was a shark and waited for the nylon trace to break, but after about 15 minutes the fish started to jump, and we realised that it was a black marlin swordfish of between 120 and 150 kilograms (265–330 pounds).

We immediately put the boat into gear and started driving away from the fish, fighting it in that way for about two and a half hours, during which time it leapt out of the water 12 times. It was Nicola's first fish and she could not fight it any more, so my friend Richard took the rod over and in about half an hour brought the marlin alongside at the back of the boat.

I leaned over the side and grabbed the trace, passing it to Richard, and moved to stick the gaff in. As I did so the marlin started to jump into the boat towards my stomach. I moved to avoid it and at first did not realise that the fish had struck me in the left side below the armpit. There was no pain, just a popping noise, but as the marlin fell back into the water I saw blood gushing from me.

The skipper packed the wound to staunch the bleeding and radioed the Narooma coastguard. It took 20 minutes to get into the harbour and an ambulance with paramedics was waiting. I had lost so much blood that during the drive to hospital my blood pressure dropped seriously and I was put on to a drip.

The marlin's serrated bill had skewered my left side and slid along my rib-cage missing my heart and lungs by centimetres, and had come out through my shoulder blade taking all the muscle tissue with it. The bill had thrust out of my back by about a foot leaving quite a hole. The wound was dirty and smelt so badly that they pumped me full of antibiotics which were continued for about a month.

The doctors said that I am very lucky to be alive. No doubt they are right, but there was a price to pay – I was unable to fish for a couple of months!

As for the marlin, it was even luckier. As I was the one most urgently in need of attention, one of the crew cut the line and let it go.

An angling injury of the same genre as that inflicted by the dead hen pheasant was described to me by Graham Rogoff, a London businessman.

While I was fishing for sailfish off Mahé in the Seychelles with four friends, sport was so good that at one point all five of us were each playing a large fish. The normal practice there, after enjoying the tremendous thrill of catching these great fighters, was to take the boat into shallow water where the boatman would throw the dead fish into the water for the waiting local people, who would wade in and take them for food. One of the anglers, Brian McGuinness, was so hot after all his exertions that he decided to dive in to cool off. As he did so the boatman was in the act of throwing overboard a sailfish, weighing perhaps 50 pounds, and the two collided in mid-air. The sharp sword went straight through Brian's shoulder, penetrating the other side.

Two of us dived in and managed to tow him ashore with the sailfish still embedded on top of him. He was conscious and we were faced with the decision of trying to pull out the sword to get rid of the dreadful encumbrance of the fish.

Fortunately a hospital was not far away and examination showed that no organs had been damaged, as they well might have been, so the fish was withdrawn. Brian soon made a complete recovery.

These were injuries inflicted by heads rather than tails but were most certainly unexpected.